A WILD
HERITAGE
The History and Nature of the
New Forest
TERRY HEATHCOTE

A WILD
HERITAGE
The History and Nature of the
New Forest

TERRY HEATHCOTE

Ensign
PUBLICATIONS

First published in 1990
Reprinted with corrections 1991
Revised edition © Terry Heathcote 1994
First paperback edition 1994

a b c d

Published by Ensign Publications
A division of Hampshire Books Ltd.,
2, Redcar Street, Southampton SO1 5LL.

All photographs by Terry Heathcote.
Cover design by The Design Laboratory.
Publisher David Graves.
Printed by Short Run Press, Exeter.

A series of 12 greetings cards based on Terry Heathcote's photographs
are also available from Ensign Publications.
Call us on 0703-702639 for the name of a stockist near you.

British Library Cataloguing in Publication Data
Heathcote, Terry 1938-
A wild heritage: the history and nature of the New Forest.
1. Hampshire. New Forest
I. Title
942.275

ISBN 185455 101 9

CONTENTS

FOREWORD

When William defined his New Forest in 1079, he had a clear purpose. Norman forest law was not developed and enforced solely to protect the coverts of the King or to preserve the Royal deer so that they were left undisturbed and cosseted for Royal pleasure. The chase was part of an infinitely more complex political and sporting strategy that allowed the King to move around his kingdom for the purpose of government and civil pacification, while at the same time catering for the sporting pleasure and stomachs of a large retinue.

The Royal forests were part of a deer hunting hierarchy that descended through the Chase, to the Warren, to the Freechase and provided hunting grounds for the nobility, lesser landowners and quite ordinary people. Norman forest law saw to it that the King's pleasure in particular, was protected by fierce clauses and awful penalties.

The needs of the Crown have altered over the centuries, but are still important and now interpreted by the Forestry Commission. A principal purpose – that of growing timber – is one of the five primary interests that are rooted in history. The five have provided, in wavering degrees of intensity, the political undercurrent since the War and are still on the agenda today. Alongside the interest of the Crown are the rights of the Commoner. These two interests have vied since William's day and perhaps before. They are the thin red line that produces the back bone of Forest history. The third major interest is public enjoyment, people drawn by the peace that wilderness brings. Tourism – today's term – has grown since the coming of the railway and increased to problem proportions, first with the car and then with the motorway. The fourth definable basic interest is that of the local people. They have their own priorities, whether they be indigenous stock, commuters or twilight settlers. The last of the five interests is the Forest's place as one of the most valuable survivals of semi-natural woodland in Western Europe. In our drained and tamed, cultivated and mono-cropped landscape, the New Forest enjoys pride of place.

Each of these five distinct interests conflict. The Commoner does not wish to see encroachment on his grazing by further tree planting or from increased wetland. The conservationist may, on the other hand, see merit in bog and coarse herbage. The local resident has mixed feelings when he returns to find a pony has munched his fuchsias or a tourist has blocked his drive.

The Forest has survived because no one of the five interests has overpowered the other. The to and fro between them has kept the balance.

Terry Heathcote gives a valuable insight into this story, whether it be man's impact on the New Forest or the rich variety of the natural environment that has flourished through history and circumstance.

The New Forest Heritage Area, renamed The New Forest Committee, now has the responsibility of conserving the wider New Forest for the generations to come. The Committee brings together the Forestry Commission, Countryside Commission, Nature Conservancy Council, New Forest District Council, Hampshire County Council and the Verderers of the New Forest in a combined effort and with a new vision. The new body

The New Forest *c.*, 1811. Map prepared by C. Smith for *Historical Enquiries Concerning Forests* by Percival Lewis.

must act with a combination of strength and sensitivity and so prove to be a significant step in the nation's effort to conserve areas of great natural beauty. The idea of such combination may well be an alternative to National Park status for other areas of 'wild heritage'.

Maldwin Drummond, O.B.E., J.P., D.L.
Chairman
New Forest Committee
October, 1990

INTRODUCTION

Situated between the Solent and Southampton Water in Hampshire, the New Forest is a marvellous survival from another age. An area appreciated for its great beauty and abundant wildlife where the centuries old practice of commoning still retains its traditional importance.

Looking round the area today with its scattering of villages and small-holdings surrounded by the open forest waste of heath, wood and bog with ponies and cattle grazing here and there, the scene remains essentially the same as some nine hundred years ago when the Forest really was new. Changes have taken place but none so dramatic as to make the area unrecognisable. The original manors at Brockenhurst, Burley and Lyndhurst have all evolved into thriving villages. Many of the once lonely tracks have been developed into roads and some areas of the open forest have been enclosed for timber cultivation. But the greater part of the unspoilt open forest waste remains.

Although thought to be rather smaller than originally, the modern perambulation or boundary, with its stock-proof fences and cattle-gridded roads, encloses an area of 93,000 acres or some 145 square miles. Almost a quarter of this is privately owned in the shape of the estates, villages and smallholdings, some having developed from original manor houses, some, such as the Beaulieu Estate, as gifts from the Crown and others by encroachment.

The remaining three-quarters, or 67,000 acres, is Crown land and originally consisted almost entirely of open forest waste. But during the last three hundred years Parliament has authorised the enclosure of some 21,000 acres for timber cultivation. Thankfully, and despite modern trends, the one hundred or so named inclosures are not entirely devoted to the cultivation of conifers but include large areas of both beech and oak. With a range of ages being allowed to develop and consideration being given to both wildlife and amenity, many of the inclosures are both interesting and quite attractive.

As a result of the development of the inclosures and of the private land over the centuries, the open forest, which was once dominant, now only covers about a half of the Forest, but even so is reputed to be the largest unenclosed area in lowland England. It is over these wastes that the commoners exercise their rights and where visitors and locals alike enjoy the open spaces and ever-changing scenery.

More often than not the Forest is thought of as simply an area of great natural beauty and a haven of peace and quiet, but it is and always has been a working Forest. Indeed, the exploitation of the area by various vested interests has not only shaped the Forest scene but has also been primarily responsible for its survival and which is likely to ensure its future.

Initially taken into Crown ownership by William the Conqueror mainly to protect the game for his own use, the interests of the Crown gradually turned from game protection to timber cultivation. Running in parallel, and often in conflict, the commoners have made use of the Forest for an equal if not longer period. Their rights have long been recognised by Parliament and are still jealously guarded, although more as a way of life these days than as an essential part of the family income as once was the case.

In addition to the interests of the Crown and the commoners, there are also amenity and conservation interests. With the Forest having been declared a Site of Special Scientific Interest, the Nature Conservancy Council has a particular interest in protecting the wildlife and their habitats. A great number of other organisations ranging from local hunts and the Caravan Club to the parish councils are also intent upon looking after their own particular interests as well as those of the Forest generally.

Although once described as 'a near miraculous survival of medieval England', jealously guarded self-interest is perhaps nearer the mark and in many ways this is reflected in the management of the Forest. The Crown lands are now technically vested in the Minister for Agriculture thus virtually making it a 'State' Forest and it is managed on behalf of the Minister by the Forestry Commission. In consequence, it is Parliament that directs how the Forest is to be managed and the Forestry Commission that carries out the work. But the Commission does not work in isolation. Parliament has also granted certain powers to the Verderers, who represent the interests of the commoners, resulting in consultation being required. Similarly, being a Site of Special Scientific Interest, the Commission is also required to consult with the Nature Conservancy Council before a range of work can be undertaken. Finally, a wide range of other interests are represented on the Consultative Panel which also makes its opinions known to the Commission.

Whether by accident or design, the various Parliamentary instructions have resulted in no individual interest having undue influence in the Forest and, though perhaps rather cumbersome, a management of reasonable equity for all.

The nine hundred years unbroken history of the Forest and use by man has, for the naturalist, produced an area of unrivalled interest and international importance. Here, habitats such as heath, ancient woods and bogs which are becoming increasingly unusual elsewhere are commonplace. The range of flora and fauna, which is arguably among the best in the country, includes many species with their main or only stronghold in the Forest and results in a year round interest.

Indeed, the story of the Forest generally is one of great interest and fascination.

THE ROYAL FOREST

The Royal coat of arms overlooking the Verderers' Hall.

In the Beginning and Forest Law

The idea of Royal Forests or hunting grounds appears to have arisen during Saxon times when the kings first decided that the Royal prerogative included the right to take over any area of previously common land enjoyed by all, for their own exclusive hunting use. Over the years a formal system of protection developed with laws to regulate their use and with officials appointed by the Crown to ensure the laws were strictly upheld. But, despite our knowledge that the Crown owned land in this area and that it was apparently used for hunting; whether or not this was why the New Forest came into being remains in doubt. All that is known with certainty is that William, Duke of Normandy, successfully invaded England in 1066 and was subsequently crowned William I, and that sometime during the following twenty years the Nova Foresta came into being.

The first mention of Nova Foresta occurs in the Domesday Book in 1086. By that time William had already taken it into Crown ownership and imposed forest law to protect the vert and venison for his own use. It was this imposition of forest law and the creation of the first Norman Royal forest that gave rise to the name of the area – and sometimes to confusion over its appearance. Today the word forest is usually used to refer to a large area of trees, but in its original sense it was a legal term referring to an area under forest law. Also, being the very first of many subsequent areas to be afforested, the New Forest really was the first or New Forest. In consequence, it also follows that Royal forests did not always – if indeed ever – consist entirely of woodland. They were invariably mixed areas containing both woods and open land, very often cultivated land and even land owned by people other than the king. In fact an area not unlike the New Forest today.

Basically forest law was designed to protect the venison – the deer – and

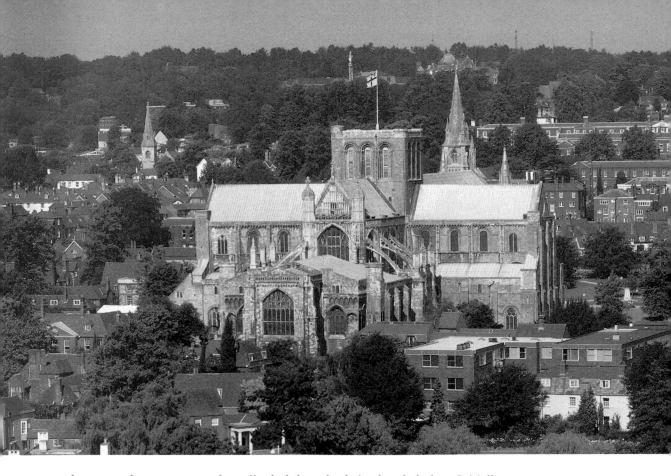

Winchester, the site of the Royal Treasury when William I created his Nova Foresta.

the vert – the greenery – that afforded them both food and shelter. Initially at least it was a very comprehensive and harsh regime, particularly for people who found themselves living under forest law. Everything was geared to the protection of the deer. Not only was killing a deer or cutting down a tree made illegal, but even the fencing of private land was not allowed in case it should interrupt the chase. Dogs above a certain size had to be 'lawed' resulting in part of their rear foot being cut off to stop them being able to run fast enough to chase down a deer. This eventually evolved into a fine being paid, in fact almost a licence, to allow a dog to remain whole. Even the few travellers passing through the Forest had to unstring their bow and strap their arrows to it, presumably to stop the temptation of taking a pot shot at a passing deer.

Indeed, so comprehensive were these forest laws that it is difficult to believe that they were something completely new when first imposed on the New Forest. Laws normally evolve in the light of experience and it does seem possible, even likely, that the laws introduced by William were modifications of previous Saxon laws or perhaps of laws introduced by King Cnut, but expanded and with much harsher penalties for contravention. Pre-existing laws might have been part of the reason why the New Forest was the first area to be afforested by William. Crown ownership of parts of the area, including the manor of Lyndhurst, and its proximity to Winchester where his treasury was situated, would doubtless also have been influencing factors.

It is similarly difficult to believe, as has sometimes been stated in the past, that William destroyed many villages and churches in creating his Forest. Domesday details the various land holdings during William's reign and during that of his predecessor, Edward the Confessor, and though there was some loss of private land, it certainly was not very extensive. With such poor, thin soils over much of the area, then as now, the Forest could never have supported a large population. Indeed a good number of people would have been required to work in the Forest and to live largely off what it could provide. With fencing being illegal, their stock would, of necessity, have been allowed to roam free. Timber to help build and repair their houses may have been allowed with perhaps peat for burning and bracken and heather as bedding for their animals – and probably themselves. It does seem logical that if the Crown needed people to help work the Forest then, despite forest laws, they would have been allowed to take the basic necessities of life from the Forest. But whether or not this was how common rights in the area first started is a totally different question. It is equally likely that these activities took place in Saxon times and were simply allowed to continue after afforestation.

But what of the purpose of the Royal Forests? Initially, in addition to providing sport for the king, the deer were also an important source of fresh meat. In days when over-wintering stock, other than the breeding animals, was very difficult and preserving meat, other than by salting, was all but impossible, feeding the king's followers, household and fighting men was of over-riding importance. In many ways it could be said that his power depended on it.

With the passing of the years and as more and more areas came under forest law – in Hampshire alone there was all or part of eleven forests – the original and commonly imposed penalties of blinding, maiming or death for contravention of forest law gradually gave way to imprisonment and fines and provided an important source of revenue for the Crown.

Being over and above the common law of the land, forest law was administered by special forest courts of which there were two, a lower and upper court. Basically, the Courts of Swainmote and Attachment initially heard all offences and, if minor, dealt with them – usually by fine. The more serious offenders were referred to the higher court, the Justice in Eyre, which periodically visited the forests dispensing justice. At least this was the intent, to visit each forest every third year. But by the fourteenth century the visits had become irregular and by the 1600s the Court visited the Forest on just two occasions. The increasing irregularity of visits was perhaps a reflection not only of the diminishing power of the Crown but also a lessening of the strict imposition of forest law – indeed generally a declining interest in deer. It also no doubt contributed to the increasing lawlessness in the New Forest at that time when the local population and many Crown officials appeared to do almost as they pleased in exploiting the area for their own benefit.

The Middle Years and Developing Timber Interests

Throughout this early period of the Forest the trees and underwood were protected by forest law, not so much for their own sake, but more as food and shelter for the deer. Despite this, a certain amount of cutting did take place. Some of it, such as the oak supplied to the royal manor house at Lyndhurst in 1297 and the timber supplied to help with the defences at Southampton in 1379 was legal, but much cutting was not. In an area where deer and stock roamed at will, natural regeneration of the timber and coppice due to browsing pressure was very poor and timber stocks were being depleted.

In 1483 an Act was passed specifically allowing parts of the Forest to be temporarily fenced or enclosed to protect the regenerating coppice after harvesting. This was the first tree-protection act ever passed and also the first indication of a change in use of the Forest from deer protection to timber cultivation. A process that was to reach its ultimate conclusion some 370 years later with the attempted eradication of the deer.

The usual type of forestry apparently practised at this time is known today as coppice with standard. Under this system the coppice or underwood was rented out by the Crown to a private tenant but always with the large standard trees scattered throughout the area being strictly reserved for the Crown. There is some evidence to suggest that a certain amount of pollarding (cutting off a tree at head height to encourage a mass of new growth) did however take place by the tenants. The enclosure that was constructed to protect the area usually consisted of a deep ditch and high inner bank, often with a split oak fence built on top and a thorn hedge planted inside. From the viewpoint of the Crown this system was most beneficial as it provided rental income whilst ensuring good protection for the valuable standard trees.

During the 1500's this system of forestry developed considerably. A survey in 1565 showed almost 6,000 acres of inclosures, whilst by the end of the century regulations were in place governing the density of the standard trees to be grown, their size before felling and extending the period of temporary inclosure to nine years. But circumstances were changing. During the 1600's the market for coppice became very uncertain resulting in the creeping neglect and abuse of the coppices. Inclosures where the banks were not already broken down were used as useful pounds for stock and other purposes, and the situation was not helped by many of the Crown officials, charged with looking after the areas, often themselves being Crown tenants of the coppices. Partially as a result of this neglect the standard trees also suffered and this at a time of growing need for large timbers, particularly for the rapidly growing Royal Navy. The amount of depredation is well illustrated by two surveys carried out at that time. In 1608 there was rather more than 120,000 trees considered suitable for navy use, but just over a hundred years later, in 1707, the number was down to just 12,000 trees. Obviously some sort of action had to be taken to remedy the situation.

In 1698 an 'Act for the Increase and Preservation of Timber in the New Forest' was passed by Parliament authorising the immediate permanent inclosure of 2,000 acres of the open forest and of a further 200 acres during each of the following twenty years, a total of 6,000 acres to be used as 'a nursery for timber'. The introduction to the Act well illustrates the previous despoliation of the temporary inclosures and of the need to ensure future stocks in mentioning that timber 'for the use of his Majesty's Royal Navy' had in the past been 'much wasted and impaired' and was 'in danger of being destroyed … unless some speedy action not be taken'.

These new inclosures, although completely free of any rights whatsoever, including common rights, were only to be developed on Forest land

A fine example of an old beech pollard in Mark Ash.

that 'could best be spared from the commons' which was no doubt of some small relief to the commoners. However there was one provision in the Act that potentially spelt disaster for both the commoners and the Forest as a whole. Once the inclosures had been established for at least twenty years and the growing trees were sufficiently large to be safe from browsing by the deer and stock, they could be laid open and a similarly sized area inclosed in lieu. This became known as the rolling powers and if taken to its logical conclusion, would have resulted in all the areas of the open forest suitable for timber cultivation eventually being completely tree covered.

At that time, thanks to the poor wording of the Act, there was some doubt as to whether these rolling powers meant just one replacement inclosure or unlimited re-inclosure to the extent of the land available. In the event, the Crown never took advantage of the provision but it did hang like a threatening cloud over the Forest for the best part of 200 years.

In addition to protecting the timber, the intention of this 1698 Act was also to rid the area of previous malpractices. In future no tree could be felled without first being viewed by an Officer or Purveyor of the Royal Navy, and if he considered it suitable for navy use the tree would be stamped with a broad arrow and crown. If the tree was then cut down or damaged in any way, the person responsible would be subject to a fine of £50 – a great deal of money in the early 1700s. Lopping or topping (pollarding) of trees by foresters, keepers or under-keepers was also made illegal and contravention not only resulted in a £10 fine and loss of employment, but also the denial of employment in any other forest. One by-product of this provision is that the great majority of the beautiful old beech and oak pollards seen around the Forest today are at least three hundred years old.

It was also considered necessary for the Act to instruct that these new inclosures were not to be ploughed, used to grow corn, used as a cattle pound or as a coppice or 'as hath late been the practice contrary to law' for charcoal burning. All of which is a very good indication of previous happenings in the inclosures. Regulations were also introduced detailing the procedures to be followed for the sale of any timber from the Forest, presumably in an effort to stop previous private enterprise by many of the Forest officials.

For all the great detail and good intentions, the Act did not prove to be very effective, at least so far as tree planting was concerned. Only 1022 acres were enclosed and planted immediately, just 230 acres planted fifty years later in 1750 and finally just over 2,000 acres in 1776. This final planting also saw the re-introduction of the Scots pine in two blocks, one at Ocknell and the other at Boldrewood. Although a native species, this was seemingly last found growing in the area at about the time of the last ice age. In view of the tremendous problems that have now developed from self-sown pines, especially on the heathlands, its re-introduction has proved to be a rather mixed blessing.

The main difficulties with these new inclosures appears to have stemmed primarily from the Forest officials, the very people charged with their care. At this time the Forest management was still mainly concerned with the protection of the deer despite the fact they produced no income and had long since ceased to be of interest for hunting by the Crown. In fact such was the number of deer that they were causing damage to surrounding estates in their search for food resulting in compensation having to be paid. The most senior official posts were largely honorary but carried the right to exploit the Forest by taking deer, timber and the like, whilst the minor officials tended to be paid so little that they also habitually exploited the area

A fine, twelve-point red stag rutting at Matley.

Queen's House, Lyndhurst, the traditional centre of Crown activities in the Forest.

Verderer's Hall, Lyndhurst, seat of the ancient Court of Verderers.

Remains of the old inclosure bank and inner thorn line at Backley Inclosure.

– mostly from necessity. And with all this being done by the supposed guardians of the Forest, it is perhaps not surprising that the local population took advantage, particularly as the Court of Swainmote and Attachment was largely ineffective and lacked proper direction.

All of these problems appear to have been recognised by Parliament thanks to various reports prepared during the 1700's. But as little was done to put matters right, it does suggest the efficiently exploited, long standing self-interest enjoyed by many of these senior officials.

An attempt to correct matters was made in 1808 with the passing of another 'Act for the Increase and Preservation of Timber'. The reason for it had altered little since the 1698 Act in that there was still 'a great and increasing difficulty of procuring a supply of timber from foreign countries, and from the estates of private individuals in the United Kingdom, for the use of the Navy'. But the wording of this new Act was again unclear. It could be interpreted as simply confirming the 6,000 acres of inclosures authorised by the previous Act or as that figure plus an additional 6,000 acres. However there was no doubt about it confirming the rolling powers and increasing the penalty for breaking down an inclosure fence to transportation for seven years after the third offence. An indication perhaps that the Crown was at last getting serious about the timber.

Uncertain though the wording of the Act was, it did not stop the authorities immediately getting further inclosures underway. They even decided to exercise their right to the rolling powers by throwing open 1022 acres inclosed under the 1698 Act and inclosing a similar sized area elsewhere. Within eight years over 5,500 acres were planted and inclosed, and during the eighteen years up to 1848, a further 1,150 acres were taken in. To the commoners looking to exercise their rights at that time, it must have been sad – if not somewhat annoying – to see, almost year by year, the open forest gradually disappearing under a securely fenced covering of trees.

Not surprisingly, for this and other reasons, relations between the Crown and the commoners had already become soured. But worse – much worse – was to come.

The Later Years and Near Disaster

To an outsider looking at the Forest at the beginning of the 1800s it must have seemed a bit of an anachronism. A management, little altered over the centuries and largely corrupt, tens of thousands of acres of open wasteland devoted to grazing by the commoners' stock and haunted by countless deer and with just a few thousand acres used for timber cultivation. Indeed a quiet backwater, perfectly content to carry on with the old ways of life. But elsewhere a revolution was under way. The open fields, commons and wastes in other parts of the country were being enclosed at a tremendous rate as more intensive agriculture developed to meet the needs of an ever-increasing population. By 1800 over 13,000 Enclosure Acts had been passed and during the next twenty years a further 1,000 were passed. England was changing rapidly from a scene that had persisted, little changed, for centuries to the now more familiar network of fields and hedgerows.

In this sort of atmosphere it is small wonder that the Crown again turned its attention to the Forest and embarked on a course that was ultimately to threaten the very existence of the area.

During the first half of the 1800's the deer continued to be a problem. From the viewpoint of the Crown their usefulness had now passed, but worse they were costing the Crown money because of the damage they caused. Even the commoners did not want them because of the competition with their stock for the available grazing on the open forest. Eventually the decision was taken that they must go and as a result the Deer Removal Act of 1851 was passed.

Doubtless many people at that time would have agreed with the introduction to the Act '...all persons having right of common or other rights in or over the New Forest, as well as other persons having estates within or adjoining to the same, would be greatly benefited by the removal of the Royal deer from the said Forest'. And many, until they reached the sting in the tail of the Act, would have been happy to continue to read that 'Her Majesty has been graciously pleased to signify her intention to give directions for the extinction or removal, with all convenient speed, of Her Majesty's deer within the said Forest, and to consent to the extinguishment of the important

Fallow and other deer were few and far between after the Deer Removal Act.

and valuable vested right of the Crown to stock and keep the said Forest stocked with deer in consideration of the compensation herein after provided in lieu of such right'.

Unfortunately, particularly for the commoners, the compensation required by Her Majesty was to inclose a further 10,000 acres of the open forest in addition to the 6,000 acres already inclosed under previous Acts. Although confirming that not more than 16,000 acres was to be behind fences at any one time, the rolling powers were still claimed which, as ever, could have eventually resulted in the Forest being completely tree-covered. It is interesting to note that it was a group of commoners that actually requested the removal of the deer and agreed to additional inclosures to the extent of 20,000 acres at most. It was subsequently flatly denied that this group represented the feelings of the commoners as a whole. But at least the inclosure limit was set at 16,000 rather than 20,000 acres.

Other than relinquishing the right to keep deer, the Act made it absolutely clear that all the other rights and privileges traditionally enjoyed by the Crown in the Forest were to be retained. And, almost in passing, made it legal for Her Majesty to grant licences 'to hunt, hawk, fish and fowl upon and over the Forest'. Today it is the Forestry Commission that grants a very limited number of such permits to the 'sporting licensees' to rough shoot over the Forest. Prior to 1851 it tended to be a favour from the Crown enjoyed by the local gentry.

Although the removal of the deer from the Forest within two years was welcomed by the commoners, the loss of further vast areas of open forest to forestry certainly was not. Neither was the other main provision of the Act, an instruction that all the common rights in the New Forest were to be registered within three months. Registration was needed because 'great doubt and uncertainty exists as to the extent of the said rights or claims, and as to the persons entitled to exercise the same'. Registration was also said to be an 'easy and economical' way of settling the claims.

On the face of it this was to the advantage of the commoners as it would put a stop to non-commoners making use of the Forest. But, as was to be learned later, the Act was much more designed to limit the value and extent of the common rights.

With the passing of the Act the Crown set about its task with vigour and within twelve months had inclosed and planted 4,000 acres. Much of the planting was of conifer and there was almost no consideration for the value of the grazing being destroyed. For the commoners and many other people the final straw came when it was learned that a letter had been sent by Mr. Cumberbatch, the Deputy Surveyor and chief Crown officer in the Forest, to his masters in London. This letter recommended that the programme of inclosures authorised by the 1851 Act should proceed as quickly as possible to limit the value of the common rights in anticipation of the day when the Forest would be broken-up.

Legal advice taken by the commoners indicated that the rolling powers assumed by the Crown meant that an inclosure could only be thrown open and a similarly sized area inclosed in its place just once. On receiving its own legal advice, the Crown insisted that the wording in the Act was meant to refer to an on-going process. That once an area had been replaced then that, in its turn, could be replaced and so on without any restriction other than not more than 16,000 acres of inclosures ever being fenced at any one time. As a result, in theory at least, no more than 16,000 acres of open forest would ever be denied the commoners at any one time. In practise however, once an area had been planted with trees and the fences eventually removed, the grazing was so limited as to be of very little use. With the introduction of iron-clad ships and consequent lessening in demand for oak, large areas of these new inclosures were being planted with conifers which made the situation even worse.

The position looked very bleak indeed – for commoners and other locals alike. The Forest was, in every likelihood, going to change out of all recognition with the traditional and much-loved scenery disappearing under a blanket of trees, most of which were likely to be conifers, and a traditional way of life and source of income was also likely to go.

The outcome was vigorous local protest, not only by commoners but many others as well. Superficially they were not a particularly influential group, especially when compared to the Crown. But the commoners included among their number not only the small cottagers and smallholders but also the powerful local landowners, many of whom were Members of

Carving in Woodfidley reputedly of the railway construction manager in 1852.

Parliament themselves and could exert influence where it mattered most. In addition, the railway had eventually reached the Forest by the late 1840's which gave the local population a small boost as well as opening up what had previously been a quiet, isolated area for the enjoyment and appreciation of a growing number of visitors. Under-estimating the great appeal of the Forest was as much a mistake then as now.

Amid all this commotion a Parliamentary committee was set up and after due consideration concluded that such were the many differences between the Crown and the commoners that the area should be disafforested and broken-up completely. A Bill to this effect even reached Parliament but was later withdrawn and a temporary ban on timber felling and new inclosures was brought in whilst matters were considered further.

In the event an alternative option was favoured, that of outlining in such great detail the respective rights and responsibilities that peace would be achieved between the Crown and the commoners. As ever in Forest affairs, this resulted in yet another Act of Parliament, the New Forest Act of 1877, which is sometimes referred to as the 'charter of the Forest' and which in many ways set the scene for the Forest we know today.

The Arrival of the Verderers, the Commission and the War Years

Under the 1877 Act a stop was put on further inclosures limiting the area to that which had previously been inclosed, some 18,000 acres, and confirming that not more than 16,000 acres could be fenced at any one time. A limit which is still applicable today. And, at long last, the rolling powers were done away with. Of equal interest, especially in these days of environmental concern, the Act also instructed that in felling trees in the inclosures 'care shall be taken to maintain the picturesque character of the ground, and not wholly to level or clear the woods, but to leave from time to time a sufficient number of the most ornamental trees'. It also instructed that the authorities should 'have regard for the ornamental as well as the profitable use of the ground'. Although having been quite widely interpreted over the years, this Act still partially governs the management of the inclosures today.

The Act dealt with the old, semi-natural woodlands, referred to for the first time as the 'ancient ornamental woods' by confirming that they were to be preserved and left open and uninclosed. The only use to be made of them was to satisfy the fuelwood rights of the commoners provided the ornamental trees were not sacrificed.

Another important action was to amend the constitution of the Court of Verderers or Court of Swainmote and Attachment. Having previously been involved for the best part of 800 years in upholding forest law on behalf of the Crown, the new role of the Court was to look after the interests of the New Forest commoners. No doubt a change, seen from some quarters at least, as the equivalent of gamekeeper turned poacher.

The Court was empowered to employ staff and to help defray expenses from a levy or marking fee on each head of stock depastured. In addition to making byelaws to regulate the rights and health of the stock generally, the Court was also given the power to 'enquire into all unlawful inclosures, perprestures, encroachments and trespasses whatsoever within the Forest … and by summary order to direct every such inclosure, perpresture, encroachment and trespass to be abated'. A power which, although seemingly innocuous, was to prove over the years either to be of great benefit in protecting the Forest or as an unnecessary hindrance to development – depending on your point of view.

This new Act was undoubtedly a victory for the commoners but it did little to end the long running disputes with the Crown. The main problem seems to have arisen because the Verderers, as a result of the Act, appeared to think that the open forest now belonged to the commoners. They tended to forget, or ignore, the fact that the Act specifically reserved all the previous rights and privileges of the Crown other than that of keeping deer. Accordingly they set about trying to establish their authority over the area.

The money received by the Crown for land lost when the railway was built across the Forest continued to be a source of conflict, whilst the Verderers also challenged the right of the Crown to allow cricket pitches on the Forest and to grant wayleaves (for access, etc.) over the open forest. This even resulted in High Court action as did the saga of the sawmills. For many years sawmills had been allowed on the open forest for use by private

Conifers such as the Corsican
pine now cover more than half
the inclosures.

contractors to convert the timber they had purchased. The Verderers
claimed, with some justification, that this was damaging the grazing and
sought compensation. The Office of Woods, predecessors to the Forestry
Commission, disagreed and this matter also ended in a High Court action.
Although it was eventually settled, it involved the Verderers in a great deal
of expense with very little to show for it. Indeed it was money they could
ill-afford from their very limited resources.

The 1914-18 war resulted in very heavy felling in the inclosures with
small regard for anything other than timber production for the war effort and
the attitude was much the same after the war when re-stocking took place.
Previous areas of broadleaf were replanted with fast growing conifers with
no regard for the amenity or anything else.

In 1924 the newly formed Forestry Commission assumed responsibility
for the Forest management and continued with the work of maximising
timber production. But there were some problems as the commoners by this
time had become used to allowing their stock to graze in many of the
previously unfenced inclosures.

This new emphasis on forestry coupled with the realisation that the
Commission had plans for the widespread conversion of broadleaf areas to
the much more profitable conifers led to considerable agitation among the
locals. Their case did appear strong particularly as the 1877 Act had specifically instructed that the 'picturesque character' of inclosures was to be

maintained and the 'most ornamental trees' retained. There were letters to the press, questions in Parliament and many a local meeting which, together, eventually resulted in a change of heart by the Forestry Commission.

Nearly 2,000 lorry loads of timber are produced each year.

In 1928 it was announced that in future, amenity was to be the prime consideration and that profit was to be secondary and an Advisory Committee was set up to 'advise the Forestry Commission as to the selection and special treatment of areas within the inclosures of the New Forest which are of outstanding picturesque interest'. This outbreak of friendly relations was continued when, some nine years later in 1937, further concessions were made by the Forestry Commission who agreed to assume responsibility for bridges and drains and for the clearance of self-sown Scots pine on the open forest. Unfortunately this new era of co-operation was bought to a halt by the outbreak of the 1939-45 war.

By the end of this war the results of almost one hundred years of lessening grazing and browsing pressures were becoming apparent. Before the 1851 Deer Removal Act deer numbers were variously estimated at between 7,000 and 9,000 head in the Forest, although perhaps half this figure might be nearer the mark. But whatever the number, their removal did allow a surge of coarse vegetation and scrub. In an effort to offset this the Crown, quite unlawfully, allowed the stock of non-commoners to graze the Forest. Following the passing of the 1877 Act this practice was continued by the Verderers, presumably for the same reason, but this time with the specific permission of Parliament. But for all that, stock numbers only averaged some 5,500 head and by the outbreak of the 1914-18 war, even this had declined to some 3,500. There was a small increase after the first war but numbers fell again during the depression years of the 1930's and, by the outbreak of the second war, only totalled some 1,700 animals. This was a very small number indeed to be feeding off the Forest especially when compared with some 5,500 stock plus a large number of deer prior to 1851. Small wonder the undergrowth was developing throughout the Forest and the grazing deteriorating.

Although stock numbers climbed rapidly during the second World War with the drive for home-grown food, the increased grazing benefits were largely offset by the lack of manpower to carry out routine Forest manage-

ment and, surprisingly, the continued suppression of the deer. War time damage did not help much either with vast areas being taken over by the military for training and airfields such as Beaulieu Heath, Holmsley and Stoney Cross. Open forest land was ploughed to grow food, whilst many gates and fences were broken down in the general mêlée. All in all it was a bit of a mess and the scene was set immediately after the war for decisive remedial action to be taken.

The Inclosure at Wooson's Hill in the heart of the central wooded area.

The Years of Change and Modernisation

The post-war years heralded a period of rapid change involving as much legislation during the following twenty-five years as had occurred during the previous two hundred and fifty years. The 'ownership' of the Forest, which is sometimes a matter of confusion even today, was settled in 1945 when the Forestry Act of that year resulted in all Crown land being vested in the

The A31 was the first main road to be fenced in 1964.

Minister of Agriculture. In consequence, the New Forest became a 'State' Forest with the Forestry Commission continuing to manage the area as before, but now in compliance with the Minister's instructions.

In 1946 the Minister appointed a committee to investigate the condition of the Forest and how best to modernise it. The committee, under the chairmanship of the Right Hon. Harold Trevor Baker, published its report – now better known as the Baker Report – during the following year. In its review of both Forest affairs and interests and in the changes recommended, it was a masterpiece of precision, fairness and common sense. Although a number of the recommendations were altered and some were not implemented at all, it did form the basis of the 1949 New Forest Act that brought about many changes still evident in the Forest today.

Membership of the Court of Verderers was increased to ten and other changes were introduced directly affecting the commoners, including the fencing of the main A31 road.

The problems of the open forest were tackled by firmly placing with the Forestry Commission responsibility for drainage, maintaining the bridges and ensuring the grazing was kept clear of 'coarse herbage, scrub and self-sown trees', but with the provision that only 'such work as appears to them after consultation with the Verderers, and with due regard to the interests of amenity, reasonably necessary, or as the Minister may direct'. Authority was also given for the temporary inclosure of open forest land for the 'cultivation and improvement of the grazing', provided that not more than 3,000 acres was fenced at any one time. In the event not much advantage was taken of this provision and even including the areas 'improved' after the war, barely 1,000 acres has even been re-seeded.

It was also this Act which authorised – for the first time – the fencing of a road in the Forest; the A31 Cadnam to Ringwood road. But it was not simply a case of putting up a fence. Compensation was paid to the Verderers for the loss of road-side grazing resulting from the fencing and a series of under-passes or creeps had to be built under the newly fenced road to ensure unhindered access to all parts of the Forest by the stock. Unfortunately the toll of road accidents involving the stock continued for a number of years after the Act as, thanks mainly to arguments over the cost, the road was not fenced completely until 1964, some fifteen years later.

Two further aspects of the Act both involved trees in one way or another, with one resulting in a change to the Forest scene and the other as a source of trouble for the future. Permission was given to the Forestry Commission to inclose a further 5,000 acres of open forest for timber cultivation subject to obtaining the agreement of the Verderers and paying them compensation for the land lost to grazing. During the 1950's agreement was obtained to develop some 2,000 acres of these 'Verderers Inclosures' as they are known, and compensation was agreed at the yearly rate of four shillings or twenty pence an acre. Today these nine inclosures can be fairly readily identified by the broad re-seeded strip surrounding them. This was included as part of the deal and intended to act as a fire break but mostly as a replacement for the lost grazing. Since that time no further inclosures have been made.

One of the other main provisions of the Act was for the regeneration and preservation of the ancient and ornamental woodlands. This allowed the Commission, with the consent of the Verderers, to make temporary inclo-sures of not more than twenty acres in extent for 'such forestry operations as appear to the Commission to be requisite'. This phrase, that seems quite reasonable, was subsequently to be given unduly wide interpretation by the Commission causing yet further difficulties.

The 1950s and early 1960s was a period, we were told, when we had 'never had it so good'. Unfortunately it was also a period when the stock in the New Forest had rarely had it so bad. Increasing prosperity coupled with a rapid rise in car ownership and mobility resulted in an unprecedented rise in road accidents involving the stock. And with the perambulation still being wide open at this time, allowing the stock to wander freely outside the Forest and with no fencing alongside any of the Forest roads, it was becoming an increasingly impossible situation for stock, commoners and motorists alike.

It was not only the stock owned by the New Forest commoners wande-ring both in and out of the perambulation that was causing problems. Stock owned by commoners with rights on many of the common lands laying adjacent to the Forest was also coming in. This tradition or custom of 'vicinage' allows stock depastured on one common to wander freely over adjacent commons and vice versa. Developed over the centuries, vicinage

The ancient woodland such as Queen's Bower has often been a source of conflict.

has the great advantage of avoiding the necessity and cost of fences between two areas of common land quite apart from arguments over trespass. But in the Forest it had one big disadvantage. Not belonging to the New Forest commoners, the adjacent commoners' stock wandering in the Forest was not subject to the byelaws of the Verderers. As a result, there was no control over their state of health, breeding or anything else, quite apart from the fact that the New Forest commoners had to pay marking fees to the Verderers whilst the adjacent commoners did not.

As ever, legislation was used to solve the difficulty and the 1964 New Forest Act resulted. The perambulation was extended to incorporate many of the adjacent commons and for the first time in 800 years the Forest actually increased in size despite some areas being disafforested in the south of the area. Part of the stock control problem was thus solved as the authority of the Verderers byelaws was extended to cover these new areas of Hale Purlieu in the north, Cadnam, Furzley, Half Moon, Penn, Plaitford and West Wellow commons in the north-east and the common lands of Hyde, Ibsley, Rockford and parts of Kingston Great in the west.

An effort was also made to limit the road accident problem with authority being given for the stock-proof fencing and cattle-gridding of the new perambulation so that at last the stock was kept in the Forest. Provision was also made for the fencing of the A35 Ashurst via Lyndhurst to Christchurch road. As almost two-thirds of the accidents had previously occurred either outside the perambulation or on the A31 and A35 roads running through the Forest, hopes were high that the carnage involving the stock might now lessen.

The rising tide of traffic and visitors was also partly responsible for another change authorised by the 1964 Act – provision for tourism. The Forestry Commission was allowed to use parts of the open forest to develop camp sites and to erect buildings as necessary for the 'health and convenience' of the campers. Although fencing of the whole site was not allowed, fencing of the buildings was. This has proved to be a mixed blessing for the campers. Many enjoy the sight of the ponies and donkeys roaming through the sites but some are not at all happy with the unerring instinct of the stock to trace food. Despite notices, some campers still feed the animals and this often results in very insistent food begging and sometimes rather bad-tempered animals who are not satisfied and at least one donkey that has learned to unzip a tent in her search for food.

Finally, in addition to recognising the growing impact of tourism for the first time, the Act also acknowledged the growing importance of the New Forest wildlife. Instructions were given that both the Forestry Commission and the Verderers 'shall have regard for the desirability of conserving flora and fauna and geological or physiographical features of special interest in the performance of their duties'.

Although perhaps anticipating some of the future developments, the 1964 Act certainly did not foresee the many major changes and upheavals that subsequently took place.

Towards the Present Day and Looking to the Future

Nature conservation was starting to play a more important role in Forest affairs and exercising an ever greater influence over the management of the Forest – sometimes to the dismay of the commoners.

In 1959 an agreement between the Forestry Commission and the Nature Conservancy Council was signed recognising the 'important nature reserve status' of the Forest, whilst in 1971 the whole area was designated a Site of Special Scientific Interest. A further agreement between the Commission and the Conservancy was signed in 1979 which resulted in even wider consultation and, in 1986, following the passing of the Wildlife and Countryside Act, the Site of Special Scientific Interest status was further strengthened. As a result of all this, consultation – both voluntary and required – takes place between the two organisations before virtually any physical management is undertaken.

However, the Nature Conservancy Council, although the leading body, is not alone in their concern for nature conservation. Local organisations including the New Forest Association, Hampshire Field Club, Hampshire and Isle of Wight Naturalists' Trust and a number of others all act in an advisory capacity and result in an influential lobbying group.

Although the growing power of the conservationists passed largely unnoticed by the public at large, the growing annual influx of tourists certainly did not. Until as recently as the early 1970s the 'open' forest was just that. And not only open to just the stock and walkers, but also to vehicles, caravans, tents and just about everything else and all practically without restriction. Vehicles ranged far and wide and managed to find the most isolated corners of the Forest whilst the more popular areas, frequented by the less venturesome, were starting to suffer badly from erosion and soil compaction. Yet again the Forest was starting to veer off course and needed to be brought back to the straight and narrow.

During the 1960s some car-free areas were created on the open forest using ditches and barrier gates, and although this was only a partial answer to the problem and disliked by many, it did gain an element of acceptance. Later in the decade a committee was established made up of representatives of all the interested authorities including the Forestry Commission, Verderers, Nature Conservancy, Hampshire County Council and the rural district councils of Lyndhurst, Fordingbridge and Ringwood. As is the way with such committees, they received opinions and comment from a whole range of individuals and other interested organisations. Eventually, in November 1970, they published a draft report 'Conservation of the New Forest' aimed, as was the Baker Report some twenty-five years previously, at 'adjusting the Forest to modern requirements'. With some 3,500,000 day visits to the Forest each year together with some 400,000 camper nights (one camper staying for one night) and an estimated 20,000 vehicles taking to the open forest at peak periods, some major adjustments were necessary.

In November 1971, following further public consultation and comment, the 'Final Recommendations' were published and shortly after, following approval by the Minister of Agriculture and agreement to meet the costs involved, work commenced. This consisted of making the whole open forest into a car-free area using the previous system of ditches, locked barrier gates and small wooden posts, usually known as dragons teeth, to keep the vehicles off. In addition, a large number of car parks were made throughout the Forest together with a series of campsites providing a range of facilities. By 1976 the work had largely been completed and the new look New Forest was established.

Set against this background of co-operation in solving one set of problems another, and equally serious threat, was developing elsewhere.

Since assuming responsibility for Forest management in 1924, the Forestry Commission had been progressively converting areas of broadleaf trees in the inclosures to the much faster growing and more productive conifers. By the early 1960's they had managed to reduce the area of broadleaf from 60% down to some 40% and for the first time to be growing more conifers than broadleaf. As if this was not bad enough, at the end of the 1960s it was learned that the Commission intended to reduce the area of broadleaf still further to just 25%. But even worse, that they also intended to start what was virtually the commercial exploitation of some of the areas of ancient and ornamental woodlands. Starting with Rushpole Wood, the intention was to heavily thin the old trees to encourage rejuvenation. Although this was just about within the 1949 Act instruction of undertaking 'such forestry operations as appear to the Commission to be requisite', it was certainly against the instructions, and spirit, of the 1877 Act. The public outcry this caused, referred to by some as the battle of Rushpole Wood, resulted in the Minister of Agriculture placing a temporary ban on hardwood felling and then visiting the Forest in 1971 to issue a mandate to the Commission detailing future management policy via the forum of the Court of Verderers.

In future the New Forest was to be 'regarded as a national heritage and priority given to the conservation of its traditional character' with the ancient and ornamental woodlands being 'conserved without regard to timber production'. In the inclosures the balance between broadleaf and conifer was to be maintained and managed with greater emphasis on amenity. Some broadleaf trees were to be allowed to grow on to an age of at least two hundred years with felling limited to single trees or small groups of not more than an acre in size.

It was during this turbulent period that the Commission established the Consultative Panel in 1970. This Panel, made up of representatives from a great range of organisations with interests in the Forest, was intended to act as a source of public opinion for the Commission and it still actively operates in this way today. Indeed when issuing his mandate, the Minister instructed that both the Panel and the Verderers were to be fully consulted on the annual programme of Forestry Commission work and, with the Commission, to comprehensively review the provisions of the mandate after ten years.

Finally in 1970 and almost lost among all the other changes, there was the New Forest Act. Its main provision was to correct an oversight resulting from the 1968 Countryside Act which gave the Commission wide powers to make provision for recreational use on land they managed. This 1970 Act added the proviso that, in the New Forest, this could only be done with the agreement of the Verderers. In addition the Act also authorised the fencing of the A337 Cadnam via Lyndhurst to Brockenhurst road, the third and last main road to be fenced.

Some ten years later in 1981, as instructed by the Minister, all these new changes were reviewed and found to be working satisfactorily. But within a few years yet another committee was established to review the Forest situation seemingly prompted, in part at least, by the growing pressures on the Forest resulting from rapid growth of many of the immediately surrounding areas. The make-up of the committee involved the same organisations as previously but included a representative from the Countryside Commission. Two working parties were set up, one to examine the 'Character of the Forest' and the other the 'Demands and Pressures'. In addition the opportunity was also taken to look at the roads and transport strategy in the Forest in an effort to limit the 150 to 200 road accidents involving the stock each year.

The 'Consultation Draft Report' published in 1987 contained, with one main exception, proposals more as minor adjustments to the working of the Forest rather than complete change. But even so, many of these produced a sharp public reaction. One suggestion was to stop the model aircraft flying at Beaulieu Heath because of the noise and intrusiveness whilst another recommended the closure of the camp sites at both Holidays Hill and Aldridgehill. In both cases the people involved organised, via their various associations, a very active campaign of objection on a national basis and even obtained the support of some Members of Parliament.

But perhaps the most radical proposal, prompted no doubt by the suggestions that the New Forest should become a National Park, was the creation of a New Forest Heritage Area Committee. The Heritage Area itself to consist of the whole of the Forest (70%) and the immediate surrounding areas (30%) much of which is a part of the Forest in spirit if not in name. An independent chairman appointed by the Government was suggested with

In the woodlands, the traditional craft of wood splitting for fencing still takes place.

Overleaf: Autumn beech in ancient and ornamental at Mark Ash.

The bank surrounding Lyndhurst old deer park, which was first recorded in 1291.

membership consisting of representatives of the Countryside Commission, Forestry Commission, Hampshire County Council, English Nature (previously known as the Nature Conservancy Council), New Forest District Council and the Verderers. The aim of the Committee would be 'to promote the conservation of the New Forest and seek co–ordinated action on issues arising in the area'.

Following publication of the consultation report, the usual period for public comment was allowed and the final recommendations were issued in 1988. After consideration by both the Forestry Commissioners and the Minister of Agriculture, final agreement to the proposals was given in March 1990. Unfortunately this document 'The Future for the New Forest' although attractively produced, was very brief at just 32 pages and at £5 tended to have a limited audience.

With some of the proposals being accepted and others not, the Report was considered a disappointment by some and a lost opportunity by others. Hunting activities in the Forest were left unaltered as was model aircraft flying on Beaulieu Heath. A number of camp sites were altered with the use of Aldridgehill being severely restricted and Holidays Hill closed completely. But the proposed New Forest Heritage Committee was enthusiastically endorsed. So much so that by mid–1990 a chairman, Maldwin Drummond, had been appointed and an advertisement placed for an officer to be employed by the Committee to co–ordinate matters. By the end of the year the New Forest Committee (as it re-titled itself) was up and running.

In 1991 the National Parks Review Panel, which had been established two years previously by the Countryside Commission, recommended to Government that the New Forest should be recognised as a National Park but with its own tailor–made constitution. In response, the New Forest Committee rejected the idea suggesting instead that special protection comparable to a National Park be given to the whole Heritage Area and that the Committee itself be given statutory status and the necessary resources.

After due consideration of the conflicting opinions, the Department of the Environment issued a consultation paper in September 1992. This broadly endorsed the opinion of the New Forest Committee but suggested that the make–up of the Committee be extended. Part of the reason for this change being that some of the proposed Heritage Area — although still not finalised — fell outside the jurisdiction of the Hampshire County and New Forest District Councils.

The suggested new Committee consists of a Chairman together with three representatives from the New Forest District Council, two from Hampshire County Council and one each from Wiltshire County, Salisbury District and Test Valley District Councils. In addition, two representatives from the Forestry Commission and one each from the Verderers, English Nature and the Countryside Commission together with three Ministerial appointments to give a total of seventeen.

Although there are many doubts locally about the proposed make–up of the new Committee — not least because of the number of local authority members — and still some differences of opinion regarding the actual size of the Heritage area, it is anticipated that all these matters will be resolved in 1994. However, with a national review of the future of local authorities currently (1994) taking place and the prospect of a unitary authority covering the Forest and, in addition, an enquiry into the future of the Forestry Commission with the possibility of privatisation, the current climate of hopeful anticipation may be short lived.

So, over the course of nine hundred years the role of the crown has changed from that of all powerful dominance to one where previously subservient subjects now themselves play a leading role. But that is not to say that the Forestry Commission is now impotent — far from it. They are still primarily responsible for the previous Crown lands in the Forest despite the system of checks and balances that has built up, almost by chance, over the years. As a result, they are unlikely (never is perhaps too big a word) to wander far from the beaten track of Forest management due to the restraint of the Verderers and English Nature or, as a last resort and as has happened in the past, the sheer pressure of public opinion. Conversely, and for similar reasons, it is unlikely that the Verderers, conservationists or indeed any other vested interest can influence the management too much in their own particular favour.

Although this system is now quite complex and seemingly a recipe for achieving little but talk, it is effective and the work of managing the Forest does get done.

THE WORKING FOREST

Oak, once the basis of power and conquest.

Making Decisions and the People Involved

The New Forest is often described as a working forest although the evidence is not always that obvious. The number of visitors to be seen around the area, especially during the summer, indicates an active tourist industry but the camp sites many of them use are largely tucked away and barely noticed. Similarly with the commoners, the stock is much in evidence but there is little to indicate who owns them let alone any sort of activity taking place. The dark green vehicles of the Forestry Commission, who are responsible for managing the area, are also regularly seen going about their business but other than sometimes hearing the distant buzz of a chain saw in an inclosure or perhaps seeing a pall of smoke over some heath, here again the signs of activity are few and far between. Yet work is taking place. Indeed the management of the Forest is a large and complex undertaking involving a large Forestry Commission staff and a budget running into some hundreds of thousands of pounds.

Based at Queen's House in Lyndhurst, the administrative centre for the Forestry Commission, the traditionally titled Deputy Surveyor has a staff of two managers, thirteen foresters, fourteen clerical staff, two head keepers, twelve keepers and some ninety forest workers in addition to a number of seasonal staff. Together they are responsible for all the commercial forestry work in the inclosures, all of the physical management of the open forest and for looking after all the recreational and conservation activities.

For the professional forester who has perhaps been university trained and worked for the Commission in other parts of the country purely involved in forestry practice and maximising timber production from an area, a transfer to the New Forest can come as somewhat of a surprise. Instead of just dealing with the harvesting and marketing of the timber and working in comparative isolation, he could well find himself organising caravan sites or perhaps heath burning or other open forest work and even worse – from the viewpoint of some – having to deal with various committees and the public generally before any of this work can be undertaken. Every element of his work will be open to scrutiny and criticism will be commonplace. Although for some this, what can best be described as culture shock, is too much and they seek to transfer out of the Forest, many enjoy the challenge despite the difficulties of holding the balance between the many interested groups in the Forest.

The needs of the commoners for grazing for their stock does not always sit happily with the needs of the conservationists for habitat protection especially when the multitude of other uses also has to be considered. And difficult though this balancing act is, the management of the area in recent years has generally worked well although not entirely without complaint. But with such a great diversity of interests it is doubtful if the Forest could ever be managed without complaints from one quarter or another. Indeed the cynic might suggest that provided all of the interested groups complain some of the time then the balance of management must be about right.

In many ways the key to the Forest management is consultation. For the open forest the largest, most used, most valued and certainly the most sensitive area there is the Open Forest Advisory Committee which is chaired by a senior Forestry Commission manager and made up of representatives from a whole range of interested organisations including the Forestry Commission, Verderers, Nature Conservancy Council, Commoners Defence Association, Consultative Panel, Countryside Commission, Ministry of Agriculture, Hampshire Naturalists' Trust, Hampshire Field Club and the Royal Society for the Protection of Birds. This widely representative Committee is also assisted by independent specialists and generally oversees the management of the whole open forest.

The more detailed planning is undertaken by three working groups each of which is again led by a Forestry Commission manager and consisting of members largely drawn from, and agreed by, the Advisory Committee. With one having responsibility for the heathland and grazing, another for the old woodlands and the third for the drainage, together they cover all aspects of the open forest physical management with the work agreed being – eventually – carried out by the Forestry Commission workers. In this way it is possible for all shades of opinion to be reflected in the management and for the various statutory requirements to be met.

In the inclosures the operations are subject to far less consultation although the Commission is required to follow the (1971) Minister's Mandate and to discuss the annual thinning programme with the Consultative Panel in addition to having consideration for the wildlife. The only exception is the areas of 'captive' ancient and ornamental woodland found in some of the inclosures. These are managed as though they were part of the open forest and are not subject to normal forestry operations.

With so much protection having developed over the years it is surprising that recently there have been suggestions that the New Forest should be designated a National Park. Rather less surprising is that most of the authorities concerned with the Forest consider this to be unnecessary which has resulted in accusations of self-interest protection.

But when the great range of protection given to the area is considered, there does appear to be little advantage to be gained from the idea. The Verderers have the statutory power to enquire into and stop any encroachment or trespass on the open forest and whilst being designated a Site of Special Scientific Interest, consultation by the Forestry Commission with the Nature Conservancy Council is required before almost any management work at all can be undertaken. The Consultative Panel, although voluntary, is similarly influential and with the bulk of the Forest being Crown land – or more correctly State land – this itself gives a particular protection.

It has been said that National Park status will help the commoners and especially any prospective decline in stock numbers. Yet this has done nothing to help the decline of stock on Dartmoor National Park or indeed the state of some of them. Planning control in the National Parks is also said to be more strict but this has not stopped military training occurring in most of them, mineral extraction being allowed and even a bypass being built across one despite a perfectly viable alternative outside the Park.

In fact these regulations do not appear to be any more effective than in the Forest where attempted strict planning control is often thwarted when locally declined planning applications are allowed on appeal to the Department of the Environment. But at least in the Forest the military were finally, and with some difficulty, removed after the last war and an application for oil drilling was thrown out some years ago. More recently, and although not welcomed by everybody, Parliament also declined to overrule the Verderers' decision not to allow the proposed Lyndhurst bypass to cross the open forest.

Irrespective of title or designation and whether controlled and guided by a Heritage Area Committee or a National Park Committee, the protection of any area ultimately rests in the hands of Parliament and the backing or otherwise given to the local organisations.

The Inclosures and Timber Production

In terms of timber production the New Forest is quite an important area in southern England although not in national terms and certainly not when compared with the vast plantations in Scotland and Wales. With some one hundred individually named inclosures covering approximately 20,000 acres, the average annual timber production is quoted as 38,000 cubic meters which is equivalent to around 2,000 large lorry loads. Doubtless this productivity could be higher but for the limitations imposed by the Minister's Mandate – although it would be at the expense of both amenity and wildlife.

Despite the progressive conversion of broadleaf trees to conifer before 1971, one of the most striking features of many of the modern inclosures is their diversity which is particularly noticeable when compared to the often monotonous tracts of conifer seen elsewhere. This diversity is helped not only by the range of species grown, often in comparatively small blocks, but also by the great range of ages to be seen.

Currently in the Forest conifers cover fifty-four per cent of the inclosures with thirty-six per cent broadleaf and ten per cent mixed broadleaf and conifer. But with the more rapid development of the conifers, these mixed areas should eventually be left as pure broadleaf and result in an almost equal balance between the two groups.

Historically, oak has been the main species grown in the inclosures and with seventeen per cent pure oak and a further thirteen per cent mixed oak and beech, this is almost the case today. In addition there are lesser areas of pure beech together with a few other broadleaf species such as the attractive stands of sweet chestnut in Backley Inclosure. In a number of the inclosures these broadleaf trees date from the 1700's making them of great value to the forester and, because they are so unusual these days, to the conservationist as well.

The Scots pine with its distinctive pale red bark towards the top of the tree, covers some twenty per cent of the inclosures and is the dominant conifer species. In many ways this is fitting as it is one of just three conifer species, together with the juniper and yew, native to the British Isles. All the other conifers found growing in the country, estimated at over 2,500 different species, having been introduced at one time or another in the past.

Following the Scots pine, the Douglas fir and Corsican pine each cover some twelve to thirteen per cent of the inclosures and are a very familiar sight. The Douglas fir was only introduced from North America in 1827 but is now a major forestry species and used for a multitude of purposes. With this species in particular there are a good number of old specimens dotted around the Forest, instantly recognised by their deeply fissured, corky bark, and which, from their size, must have been planted within a few years of being first introduced. The Corsican pine is a much older introduction dating from the 1700s and with its liking for light, sandy soil is well suited to many parts of the Forest.

The Norway spruce, introduced in the 1500's and perhaps better known as the Christmas tree, is grown in a number of areas. The Sitka spruce, with its preference for wetter soils can also be found in a few areas and together these two species cover some five per cent of the inclosures. Among the other species found in noticeable quantities are the larch, particularly the Hybrid Larch a cross between the European and Japanese. This is unusual in casting its needles during the winter and is especially attractive in the Spring as the yellow male and red female flowers appear and, a little later, the bright green tufts of the new needles. Western hemlock, arguably the most graceful of all the conifers, is also to be found and seemingly in increasing quantities. In addition there is quite a range of other conifer species planted throughout the inclosures adding to both the interest and variety.

With such a great variety, large scale stock maps are an absolute essential. These maps maintained by the Commission show not only the various species, date planted and size of area, but also the various compartments, sub-compartments, gravel tracks and the rest. All information which is needed to manage the inclosures and to plan the planting, thinning and felling programmes.

Once an area has been felled, restocking takes place either in the form of planting, natural regeneration or a combination of the two. For planting the ground is often prepared by a scarifier, a large Scandinavian produced machine reputedly costing £100,000, which breaks down the matted accumulation of needles and branches. Such is the power and effectiveness of these machines that only two are required; one covering Scotland and the other covering all the Forestry Commission plantations in England and Wales. In consequence, preparing the comparatively limited areas to be

Ride damage is an inevitable temporary result of winter forestry work.

planted in the New Forest only requires a visit of a week or so each year.

With all the tree nurseries in the Forest now having been closed, the seedling trees are brought in from outside for planting between October and April. The conifers are grown in small, six inches high, degradable paper containers and are planted at a distance of some two metres from each other giving a planting density of rather more than 900 to the acre. Usually these newly planted areas are fenced to give protection against the deer and other damage, but sometimes the large white plastic bags which originally contained the trees will be seen suspended from branches around the area. Gently swinging in every little breeze, this seemingly crude but quite effective arrangement is also designed to keep the deer away – at least for a short while.

In contrast to the conifers, broadleaf seedlings are invariably planted in protective plastic tubes known as single tree shelters or Tuley tubes after the Forestry Commission employee who first developed them. Usually about five feet high and some five to six inches in diameter, they act almost as a mini greenhouse to help promote rapid growth whilst also giving protection against deer, rabbits and all the other creatures which tend to regard seedling trees as a tasty snack. Indeed since the introduction of this system, such has been their effectiveness that there barely seems to be a broadleaf tree planted anywhere in the country without the benefit of a tube.

The power of the scarifier preparing the ground for planting.

Children's delight – fire fighting demonstration at a Forestry Commission open day.

Controlled heath burn in February, at Castle Hill, Burley.

Timber production remains an important part of Forest life.

Right: The tattered remains of an inclosure, near Mogshade Hill, after the storm of January 1990.

Contractor removing newly felled timber from an inclosure.

Fields, once part of a commoner's holding, now often used to graze riding ponies.

Bridge over Shepton Water – one of many maintained on the open forest.

Although some care of the young trees is required for a few years after planting, once established they develop rapidly resulting in the conifers requiring thinning after fifteen to twenty years. Further thinnings are taken periodically and depending on soil conditions and other factors, the trees are finally felled after fifty to sixty years although in some selected areas the period is extended to 120 years. A similar procedure is followed with broadleaf but, as a result of the Mandate, felling takes place after 200 years rather than the more usual 120 years as is the case elsewhere for broadleaf. And it is also for this reason that the broadleaf trees are only felled either individually or in small groups of not more than an acre in extent.

To ensure continuity of work for the foresters, an even flow of various aged timber and for wildlife considerations, the Forest is divided into five working blocks consisting of areas scattered throughout the inclosures with each of these blocks being worked for one year in turn. And it is also for wildlife considerations that broadleaf felling only takes place during the winter months.

Despite the work being almost continuous, modern machinery such as the scarifier before planting, chain saws for thinning and felling and machines for extracting and eventually removing the timber, results in surprisingly few men being required for what, on the face of it, is a big operation. Evidence of felling in the shape of timber stacked at the ride side is more often noticed than the work itself although nearby the stumps will have a blue-green tinge indicating that they have been newly felled and painted with a fungicide to stop the development and spread of conifer heart rot.

The stacks of various aged timber are all sprayed with a reference number and initials to indicate the contractor who has purchased it and although sometimes seeming quite small, all the timber does have a use. The smaller wood will be used variously for stakes, posts and pulp whilst the larger wood, from some six inches in diameter and above, is suitable for saw logs. This smooth flow of timber fetching reasonably consistent prices can be seriously disrupted by storm damage. Clearing up the damage, making public areas safe, repairing fences to stop stock wandering and all the other unexpected work can severely upset the planned work programme quite apart from the glut of timber causing prices to fall.

In addition to experiencing severe storm damage, the Forest is also helping to mitigate it with some selected stands of mature trees being used as a source of seed. Until very recently this has been collected by hand with the Forestry Commission staff involved being helped by volunteers paid by weight collected. With such large quantities being required – quite literally acorns and other seed by the sackful – it is a job requiring nimble fingers and in some areas of the country school children help with the work. In the Forest in future, it has been decided that the work will be done by contractors. But whoever collects the seed, following the recent storms millions will be required to keep the nurseries stocked and eventually replace the countless trees lost.

Activity in the inclosures is not entirely associated with timber production. The gravel rides have to be developed and maintained to be sufficiently strong for the weight of the fully loaded timber lorries as indeed do the bridges over the culverts and streams. Similarly the culverts and streams themselves need to be maintained to ensure satisfactory drainage. The often extensive ride damage resulting from timber extraction, particularly during the winter, needs to be put right, whilst the fences and gates also have to be kept up to scratch. With modern fences being made of wire strand or mesh, this is a far easier job than in the old days when inclosure boundaries were much more substantial. Previously a deep ditch was dug and the earth thrown up into a bank behind and a split oak fence built on top very similar to the fence now surrounding the grounds of Queen's House.

In addition to many of these old boundaries surviving, some of the old types of forestry are also making a comeback with hazel coppicing at Pond-head Inclosure and sweet chestnut coppicing at Haseley Inclosure. There is even a small amount of experimental pollarding. New oak pollards can be seen at Great Linford Inclosure and holly pollards at both Matley Wood and Backley Wood. Although both these old forestry practices are on a very small scale, it does help add yet another element of interest to an already diverse scene.

Managing the Heath and Open Areas

In contrast to the management of the inclosures, the work involved in maintaining the open forest is far more wide ranging. This reflects the differing types of area involved and also the much greater range of interests including both commoning and conservation.

Although looking natural, the heathlands are the product, and indeed owe their continued existence, to the work of man. Thought to have arisen following the clearance of the original woodlands some thousands of years ago, the heathlands appear to have persisted as a result of exploitation and possibly accidental fires. Until comparatively recently turf was dug extensively by the commoners in addition to taking both bracken and gorse, whilst the stock and the deer have both made use of the area over the centuries. Today the heathlands are extensively managed to stop the natural reversion to woodland in addition to ensuring adequate grazing for the stock.

The most widespread of the unwanted vegetation occurring on the heaths is the self-sown Scots pine. More accurately it is the young self-sown pine that is so disliked because of its potential to shade out the heather and any other vegetation. The mature pines, sometimes seen as individual trees and sometimes as small clumps, are valued by many as adding an element of interest to an otherwise apparently barren scene. And this is the main source of the problem. In consequence of the mature trees being left to avoid public reaction to their removal, the control of the young self-sown trees is a constant and costly problem. So great is the work involved that in recent years local voluntary conservation groups have been assisting with their removal. Although few would like to see the attractive mature pines completely removed from all the heathland, the cost of retaining them does seem to be high.

The Forestry Commission's requirement to maintain the biological diversity of the Forest can also result in tree control around the edges of some of the woodland areas where there is a tendency for it to gradually spread over the heathland. The pioneering Scots pine and birch are the usual species that do need an element of control. Despite the Scots pine having become so commercially important since its reintroduction to the Forest in the 1700's, it is tempting to wonder if the cost of controlling the unwanted trees on the heathland does not sometimes outweigh the profit made on those grown in the inclosures.

Another plant involving regular expenditure of both time and money is the ragwort, a bright yellow flower growing some two feet high. When it starts to wilt it becomes poisonous to the stock so its removal is more a safety measure than for any harm it may do to the Forest. All the removal is by hand-pulling, usually during August, which is a job as arduous as it is back-breaking – especially in a hot summer when the ground is iron-hard. To the forest workers involved it must be particularly disappointing to see so much ragwort left on private land around the Forest being allowed to seed and thus perpetuate the problem.

In contrast to the sheer hard work involved in limiting the Scots pine and ragwort, science is now helping to control the spread of bracken. Although resisted for many years because of possible damage to the flora and fauna, bracken spraying commenced on an experimental basis in the late 1980's with the newly sprayed areas being fenced and suitably signed. Early evidence indicates that this is a most effective method of control with no ill-effects being noted in other plants or animals, including the stock. Accordingly the programme is to be extended during the 1990s concentrating on bracken invading areas of heathland. As ever, there is close liaison by the Commission with both the Verderers, because of the stock, and with the Nature Conservancy Council because of the wildlife interest and most particularly because of the wild gladiolus. This very rare plant which is now only found growing in parts of the New Forest is mainly associated with the bracken areas, and for this reason alone the bracken will never be completely eliminated from the Forest.

Although few will be sorry to see the areas of bracken decline, the same is not entirely true of the rhododendron. This shrub is becoming as invasive in the Forest as in some other parts of the country and an effort is now being made to control its spread. Cutting and burning are the preferred methods, but whether this will prove to be completely successful remains to be seen. Like the pine, it does shade out all the other vegetation and this great disadvantage more than offsets the few glorious weeks of colour each year.

The control and management of the heathlands also involves the maintenance of a healthy covering of heather which mainly takes the form of burning. This method of management can also cause controversy particularly when it occurs in areas which are especially popular. But it is necessary for a variety of reasons. It helps to remove much of the scrubby vegetation trying to become established on the heathlands and it also promotes healthy new growth of both heather and gorse. In addition, and for the commoners most importantly, it results in a good flush of grass which is greatly welcomed by the stock.

The areas to be burnt or cut each year are decided by the Working Group and are selected from suggestions made by the commoners, keepers and other interested people. The decision as to whether to cut or burn is made mainly on the grounds of safety: the proximity of roads, woodlands, etc. Although the aim is to control some fifteen hundred acres each year, representing about five per cent of the total heathland, the actual amount

achieved is very weather-dependant. By law, burning in the south of England can only take place in the winter months from October to the end of March mainly because of wildlife considerations. In consequence a wet winter can disrupt the programme or result in some poor and not very effective burns. Following particularly bad winters, it is sometimes possible for the authorities to obtain permission to extend the burning season for a week or two beyond the end of March, but this is disliked because of the dangers to the heathland wildlife. Indeed in years when there is an early spring even burning during March does not seem very appropriate.

Burning is not always entirely beneficial as, despite every effort, burns

Controlling a controlled burn needs skill and experience.

Scots pine, attractive when mature but the source of unwanted seedlings.

do occasionally get out of control and if anything, this potential danger is even greater today than previously. Modern conservation pressures have resulted in a much greater number of small areas being burnt compared to the old days when the areas were much larger and, in consequence, the number of burns needed each year was fewer. A patchwork of small burns spread throughout the heathlands is undoubtedly better for the wildlife and is certainly much less of an eyesore, but a greater number of burns does give a correspondingly greater chance of one of them going wrong. Even with teams of at least six men, on-site water carriers and radio contact, a sudden change in direction and strengthening of the wind can cause difficulties – although this is remarkably rare.

Perhaps sometimes controversial, burning is still the most effective method of heathland control and it is fortunate that the heathlands in the Forest are of sufficient size to allow this to happen.

Douglas fir, a quick-growing, straight-grained conifer.

Work on the Wetlands and the Old Woods

The wetlands, which are among the most natural features of all in the Forest, also require a certain amount of maintenance. But as with many of the other areas, minimum intervention is the rule.

With well over one hundred miles of streams with many of them passing through woodland areas, winter gales resulting in fallen trees and branches can cause problems. A fallen tree or large branch in a stream catching all the floating debris can, sometimes within a few weeks, develop into a quite effective dam and without regular clearing, up-stream flooding, bank erosion and other troubles can occur. However it is unusual for other stream control work to be undertaken such as bed deepening or bank grading to completely eliminate flooding, as in some circumstances an element of flooding is actually required.

The alluvial or stream-side lawns which are so favoured by the stock as grazing areas, need regular flooding for their continued productive existence. During heavy winter rains the rush of water and rapidly rising levels in the streams often spills over the banks onto the surrounding lawns. As the water spreads out and the speed of flow slackens, this allows silt carried in the water to be deposited on the lawns where it acts as a fertiliser and results in these areas being the most grass productive of all in the Forest. This works well providing the water freely drains back into the streams as their level falls. If not, the standing water will result in boggy conditions developing and degradation of the grazing. Drainage ditches and channels criss-cross many of the lawns to ensure this free drainage, whilst out of sight underground there is often a complex network of pipes and soakaways.

Streamside lawns such as Longwater are important grazing areas.

The regular maintenance or otherwise of these drainage networks has often proved to be an area of controversy in the past – and sometimes even today. Claims have been made that some of the modern boggy areas were once lawns that have been lost through lack of drainage. On the other hand, conservationists are usually keen to preserve all the bogs because of their wildlife interest. In the past this has resulted in some major drainage schemes which have proved to be of doubtful value. But nowadays, with thinking having changed, further major schemes are most unlikely.

Safe access to the open forest also requires a good number of bridges and causeways over the streams and boggy areas. Although many of the bridges are only required for foot traffic, some are needed for vehicle access and all need regular checking. Being constructed of wood, they readily rot in these damp situations whilst winter flooding can undermine the supports.

The final aspect of open forest work involves the ancient and ornamental woodlands where the main cause for concern is the lack of satisfactory regeneration in some areas. The main reason for this is generally attributed to excessive grazing pressure by the deer and stock but this does not really explain how these old woodlands have managed to survive the centuries with

Although largely self-regenerating, help is required in some old woodlands.

The modern keeper's work includes monitoring birds and other wildlife.

Right: A young tawny owl, one of a number of species regularly monitored.

The deer sanctuary at Boldrewood, a popular place to see the fallow deer.

The Lymington River at Brinken, part of over a hundred miles of streams in the Forest.

Regular daily feeding encourages the deer to use Bolderwood.

little or no interference from man. However there is evidence to suggest that there is a surge of regeneration whenever stock numbers are particularly low and no doubt with patience this situation would occur again at sometime in the future. But modern thinking is that some thirty per cent of the old woodlands are not self-regenerating satisfactorily and that something must be done to remedy the situation.

Various methods have, and still are, being tried with varying success. In the past clumps of trees have been planted and fenced during their initial development. But when the fence is removed they tend to look just what they are – clumps of trees artificially introduced – and completely out of place in otherwise natural surroundings. Similarly in the past, areas have been fenced and left for nature to take its course in anticipation that, with the lack

of grazing, trees will develop. To date only a dense growth of silver birch has developed but this could well provide protection for oak and beech to grow in the future.

Interpretation of the forest is becoming increasingly important.

    More recently individual trees have been planted with their own little wire fence as protection. Ultimately these will be much more in keeping with their surroundings but over the years they do tend to be forgotten and the often tangled remains of the wire fence can become a nuisance to the stock and dogs. Perhaps in time a different type of fencing will be tried for this most suitable but rather time consuming method of replacing lost trees. Recently in some areas, as an experiment, the ground has been broken up by the scarifier, fenced, and then planted with acorns. But with being so slow growing, the fence will be needed for many years until the trees are free from potential browsing. An alternative method which avoids the need for fencing and which dates back many hundreds of years is to sow the acorns together with thorn berries. In this way the quicker growing thorns provide browsing protection for the slower oaks. This system could perhaps better be described as the natural method rather than being traditional. In many of the old woodlands where trees have fallen for one reason or another and a gap in the canopy has developed allowing in more light, thorn, holly and especially bramble readily develop and give protection to oak and beech seedlings which germinate by chance under their cover. Given sufficient time, these glades no doubt ebb and flow almost like the tides although on a time scale of decades or centuries rather than years.

Generally, the open forest work is quite successful in striking a balance between the needs of the commoners, conservationists and other interested groups whilst at the same time retaining the traditional character of the area. Indeed in one sense it could be said to be too successful as it does result in yet further work – that of recreational control.

Recreation, Conservation and the Keepers' Work

The great surge of work – and expenditure – involving recreation and conservation occurred during the 1970's with the development of the car parks, caravan sites and making the open forest a car free area. But that is not to say nothing has been done since.

Facilities at some of the camp sites are quite extensive with showers, toilets, razor points and all the other modern requirements being supplied including electrical hook-ups at two sites, whilst even the most informal sites have a water supply and provision for waste disposal. All this requires considerable maintenance and a sizeable staff of summer wardens to look after the sites. The car parks need to be regularly re-surfaced with the toilets and rubbish bins attached to many of them being serviced, usually on a daily basis. The removal of rubbish and waste from the caravan sites, car parks and Forest generally is a major undertaking. Contractors are employed to remove wet waste and others for the dry waste, whilst the Commission themselves carry an estimated 1,000 cubic metres of rubbish from the Forest each year. But even this is not enough as a regular 'clean-up' week needs to be organised each year with volunteers helping to collect litter and other rubbish left in odd corners of the Forest by people who seem to treat the area as a vast refuse tip. And with garden rubbish being involved among a surprising range of other things, it is not always the visitors who are responsible.

With many not appreciating that the Forest is now car-free, and some not choosing to, the dragon's teeth and road side ditches need regular repair, although this does little to deter some of the motor bikes and even the odd four-wheel drive vehicle.

On the basis that a greater understanding and appreciation of the Forest will result in more considerate use, a good deal of effort is put into publicity and explaining how it all works. Every year a large number of guided walks are organised and led variously by Commission staff and local people with a specialist knowledge of the area and, more recently, by a full time summer guide specifically employed for the purpose. These walks are mainly based on the various caravan sites with some from Lyndhurst, and provide a good opportunity to explain what the Forest is all about. Similarly, various way-marked walks have been developed and with leaflets and static signs, this again allows the working of the Forest to be explained.

The Forestry Commission stand at the New Forest Show is usually large and attracts thousands of visitors each year. Although time consuming to organise, this also provides an ideal vehicle for Forest interpretation – not to mention publicity for the Commission.

Rather less well known, but likely to become a regular feature because it is proving so popular, is the Commission's Open Day which is held every second year in one of the inclosures. With a whole range of active displays and demonstrations covering all aspects of Forest work, it does provide a most interesting insight whilst again promoting a better understanding.

This whole area of publicity and interpretation has now become so important that it is likely a full time official will be appointed by the Commission purely to deal with this aspect of the Forest.

Dealing with the public and involvement with conservation is also be-coming an increasingly important part of the great variety of work undertaken by the New Forest keepers. Their traditional work with deer including both census and selective control still continues as does the regular control of vermin, but this is just about all he has in common with estate keepers. These days in the New Forest the keepers need to be skilled naturalists and have a thorough knowledge of the wildlife on their beat in addition to carrying out their regular patrols and maintaining contact with the public. With anti-poaching patrols, attending the hunts, assisting with the various shows and a wealth of other duties, the modern Forest keeper's life is busy although thanks to vehicles and radios, perhaps not quite so hard as previously.

It is evident from one keeper's diary that has survived from the 1860s that their life used to be harsh in the extreme. Days off were a great rarity and holidays non-existent. Even one Christmas Day in 1866 the keeper, Harry Cooper, recorded 'To Ances Wood killed nine squirrels. To Bolder-wood After'. Whilst some months later in a similarly matter of fact way, he records 'My poor wife died this morning. To Sloden Wood'. On the day of her funeral only a couple of hours were spared before resuming his patrols. And so life went on, day after day, with the only relief being occasional visits to Lyndhurst to practice with the volunteer rifle brigade.

But harsh though life was for the keepers, it was not much different for the so-called vermin. In one month alone he records killing 'seventy-two jays, twelve magpies, eight hawks, two crows and one self-hunting dog'. With some twelve keepers operating in the Forest at that time, the annual cull must have been very great, and it is not surprising that 'hawks' became quite rare. And all this did not include the countless rabbits and squirrels – all red squirrels at that time – which were killed on a regular daily basis.

Undoubtedly conditions are far better for those working in the Forest today, but whether the same could be said for the appearance of the place and the wildlife is open to question by some.

Highland cattle are very much at home in the occasional snow.

THE COMMONER'S FOREST

H¹	ℝ	⊥ᴾ	DB
W̄	B7	FAB	F3
ꓱ	FV	Ⓢ	PT
Ⓗ	DOC	ꓲ	C7

The commoners' brands are many and varied.

Gradual Development and Changing Fortunes

Common rights, which were once widely exercised throughout the country, date from a period long before the Norman Conquest and seemingly evolved to help meet the necessities of life: the need for food, shelter and warmth. Typically, a small village or hamlet owned by the Lord of the manor and with cultivated fields nearby, would have been surrounded by waste or uncultivated land which was available by all for use in common. Then, as now, it allowed one person to take or make use of the natural produce of land owned by another. Exactly what could and could not be done, the rights, were invariably specified and typically included the right to turn out stock of various types, to take wood, to exploit the soil for peat, sand or gravel and, in some areas, to take fish. The system persisted for many centuries with little change until the Enclosure Acts of the seventeenth and eighteenth centuries and although some areas of common land did escape, few are nowadays exploited to any great extent by commoners.

The New Forest is now one of the few areas in the country where this ancient system of agriculture is still extensively practised and is also said to be one of the very few, if not the only area, where statutory recognition has been given to the commoners. Possibly of even greater importance has been the shaping of the Forest by the practice of these rights, particularly the grazing of stock, which has resulted in a unique landscape that is still dependent on depastured stock to maintain its traditional character. Without the pressures of grazing it is doubtful if physical management by man alone could stop the natural progression of many of the Forest areas to woodland. Indeed, without the commoners' jealous protection of their rights, it is doubtful if the Forest would have survived at all. But changes have taken place especially with the areas available to the commoners.

Throughout the centuries the amount of open forest waste, where the commoners exercise their rights, has been gradually reduced. In the early days of the Forest, land was lost to encroachment and as a result of gifts by the Crown, whilst from the end of the seventeenth century progressively larger areas were lost to inclosure. More recently roads have been fenced and the stock has been confined to the Forest with the resultant loss of road side and other grazing which was traditionally exploited outside the perambulation.

Although the commoners have been subservient to the interests of the Crown throughout much of the Forest's history, firstly to the deer and then timber cultivation, during the last hundred years there have been more positive aspects. The Verderers' Court has been reconstituted to look after the interests of the commoners and their rights and today is a powerful and

All the common rights are registered to land and property.

influential body with their activities and decisions not only affecting the commoners, but the Forest as a whole. But for all the modern era of co-operation and consultation between the commoners and the Crown, there still remains a lingering element of mistrust among some of the commoners based on past injustice, and doubts about the future of the Forest resulting from changing use and emphasis. Looking at the past, this attitude by some can be appreciated.

In the early days of forest law when the deer were of paramount import-ance and the very reason for the Forest's being, all the stock had to be removed from the Forest for more than six months of every year. During the 'fence month' which lasted from 20 June to 20 July – fifteen days either side of the old midsummer day – the stock had to be removed in case they interfered with the deer whilst they were dropping their young. To the commoners involved with removing their stock this was no doubt more an inconvenience than hardship for such a comparatively short period. But far more serious was the 'winter heyning' which started on 22nd November and lasted throughout the winter until 4th May. This time stock removal was required to avoid competition with the deer for scarce winter feed. This would undoubtedly have caused problems, if not hardship, particularly in those early days before the widespread storage of winter feed. These two periods did have the effect of limiting the number of stock an individual commoner could turn out to the number he could keep on his holding during the fence month and winter heyning. To stop any commoner taking undue advantage, some sort of limit has seemingly always been enforced on all common land. The usual restriction was known as levancy and couchancy – literally, standing up and lying down – which limited the number of stock turned out on common land to the number levant and couchant – which could be held – on the commoners own land.

Although still law, there were long periods, especially as the Crown's interest in deer gradually declined, when fence month and winter heyning were not strictly enforced and the stock was allowed to wander undisturbed throughout the year. Then, and no doubt much to the commoners' surprise, with the passing of the Deer Removal Act in 1851, the Crown decided once more that fence month and winter heyning were to be fully enforced. Perhaps incensed might be a better description particularly as the Act, among other provisions, resulted in the Crown giving up the right to keep deer in the Forest and indeed authorised their complete destruction and removal. In other words, a situation where the commoners were required to remove their stock from the Forest for long periods in case they should interfere with the non-existent deer. Small wonder the commoners did not like it. There is a temptation to think of this renewed imposition as sheer awkwardness on the part of the Crown, but more likely it was simply a way of stressing that, although the right to keep deer had been relinquished, all the other rights and privileges enjoyed by the Crown in the Forest were being retained. In addition, and perhaps more likely, it was an attempt by the Crown to diminish the value of the rights in anticipation of the complete break-up of the Forest and its subsequent division between the Crown and the commoners.

But for whatever reason, the uproar resulting from this and other griev-ances eventually achieved success when, in 1877, fence month and winter heyning were finally abolished. Or at least abolished in practice but legally

only suspended. The Crown agreed not to impose them 'in consideration of a payment to Her Majesty by the Verderers on behalf of the commoners a sum of twenty shillings on or before the 14th January every year as an acknowledgement of the absolute right of Her Majesty to enforce the fence month and winter heyning'. Today, as a result of this, stock can be found on the Forest throughout the year.

The Act of 1851 resulted in another unwelcome change for the commoners; the registration of all common rights. Instructions were given that all commoners claiming rights on the Forest had to submit a written application, virtually for consideration, and that a rights register would be published

Sometimes described as the architects of the Forest.

within three months. In the event this time scale was overly ambitious, partly as a result of the uncompromising attitude of the committee appointed to sit in judgement and partly from the various appeals that resulted. The Register of Claims was eventually published in 1858.

Of all the claims submitted by individual commoners and by landowners on behalf of themselves and their tenants, around one-third were completely disallowed apparently without any reason being given. Of the 863 claims that were allowed, each one was amended to a greater or lesser degree. There was not one claim allowed in full and this, coupled with an unknown, but thought to be large, number of claims not submitted for various reasons resulted in the common rights in the Forest being, if not decimated, then certainly reduced.

The Register was published in book form with the information tabulated in some detail including the claim number; name of commoner applying; whether the claim was allowed, disallowed or amended together with the date; the type of claim allowed and finally, the details of the land and property to which the rights attached together with the tythe map number. All told some 2,082 rights were registered from the 863 amended claims finally allowed.

With the passing of the years, declining use of tythe map numbers and consequent increasing difficulty in using the Register, Parliament in 1949, instructed the Forestry Commission to transfer all the information to large scale Ordnance Survey maps. These were bound into a series of volumes known as 'The Atlas'. This has since been extended to include the rights associated with the adjacent commons which were brought under the authority of the Verderers following the 1964 New Forest Act.

In the Atlas each property and plot is given a reference consisting of a series of numbers over letters. The numbers above indicate the original tythe map number, whilst the letters, if any, below, indicate the type of right registered to the plot or property. These properties with rights attaching are not always restricted to the Forest itself. Some are to be found as far away as the edges of Bournemouth, Salisbury and Southampton and even well into Dorset, at Cranborne. And it is this fact that has led to speculation that in the past the Forest once covered a much larger area.

The Atlas, a copy of which is at Queen's House, now regulates the commoning in the Forest where all the rights attach to property rather than to individuals. And it follows that anyone moving into the area and buying or occupying a property can easily check with the Atlas to see if any rights are attaching and if so, they can take advantage of them if they are so inclined. It also follows that if the occupier moves for any reason, then it is the new occupier that enjoys the benefit of the rights.

This does have some disadvantages when a property is taken over as not everyone is interested in commoning. But of even greater concern is the tremendous escalation in price of many of these properties putting them well beyond the reach of potential commoners – especially the children of existing commoners who, after all, have the right background.

Of the six rights available in the Forest and indicated in the Atlas – O = Marl, T = Turbary, S = Sheep, F = Fuelwood, M = Mast and P = Pasture. Not all of these are attached to each and every property, some have the benefit of a single right, whilst others have more and many none at all. Generally the rights of fuelwood and turbary will be found attaching to property with the other four usually associated with land.

Although today the economic importance of common rights has declined somewhat, historically and until comparatively recently, they were exercised extensively and were very important. They allowed local land-owners to charge a rather higher rent to tenants for property with the benefit of rights, whilst at the other extreme, to the cottager, rights often repre-sented the difference between a life of unremitting hardship and one of relative comfort. Indeed the common rights enhanced the standard of living generally. Today, changing circumstances – particularly financial – have resulted in an increasing number of commoners exercising their rights much more as a traditional way of life rather than for any great financial benefit. Few, if any, have to rely on them. But that is not to say that there has been any lessening of the value of the rights. The modern commoners are as intent upon protecting their inheritance as ever, which can only be for the continuing good of the Forest.

Rights of Marl, Turbary and Sheep

The modern rights fall broadly into two categories with three still being actively exercised and the remaining three largely having fallen into disuse.

The common of marl is now just a memory with traces of its previous importance to be seen dotted around the Forest. Marl is a type of lime-rich clay that outcrops particularly in the south of the Forest and which at one time was extensively dug and spread on the fields as a fertiliser. With the soils often being quite light and acid, this was no doubt of great value before the days of cheap artificial fertilisers. Of the twenty-three marl pits once in use, most are now barely recognisable having become overgrown with trees or flooded over the decades. But they are far from all being just abandoned holes as a number have evolved into quite attractive features, some suppor-ting wildlife found nowhere else in the Forest. Hatchett Pond, a favourite with visitors and locals alike, was once a series of marl pits, whilst tucked away in Hollands Wood both frogs and toads take early spring advantage of a shallow flooded pit. With interesting flowers at some and dragonflies at others, they have proved to be an unexpected benefit over the years.

Although one or two are mentioned on modern maps, a complete list was given in the 1858 Register of Rights together with the name of the keeper's beat or walk. (See Appendix III.)

The common of turbary is the right to dig peaty turf from the heathlands for burning at home and, although at one time very important, this again is now rarely exercised. The main decline appears to have occurred during and immediately after the 1914-18 war as a result of the rapid growth of motorised transport coupled with the ready availability of cheap coal. In its heyday turf became the main local fuel and it was cut in almost unbelievable quantities. With some hundreds of commoners benefiting from the right and each cutting on average about four thousand turves a year, the quantity taken from the Forest was counted in millions.

The traditional or accepted method was to cut one turf and leave two to

At East Boldre a memory of the importance of the common of turbary.

allow for quicker regrowth and to leave some grazing for the stock. But the usual practice was not always followed and with the amount of extra work this involved, it is not really surprising. This misuse was probably made worse because many, if not most, of the commoners had the turves cut for them by semi-professional turf cutters who would doubtless have been much more interested in getting the job finished as soon as possible rather than bothering about usual practice. Another factor could well have been that with turbary rights usually being attached to property and pasture rights to land, the commoner cutting turf did not have the right to turn out stock anyway and human nature being what it is, they also did not bother unduly.

The third of these little used rights is the common of sheep. This right attaches to very few properties being mainly restricted to the Beaulieu Estate, some areas along the western edge of the Forest and a small area in the north at Godshill, all of which originally had some sort of monastic connection. Records of sheep on the Forest are sparse which is probably because numbers have never been very large and for long periods there have been no sheep at all.

In the 1200s the monks at Beaulieu Abbey are recorded as having sold twenty-five sacks of wool which presumably came from sheep grazed on the Forest, whilst in 1878 a census of stock on the Forest noted 438 sheep depastured. But this appears to have been a not particularly successful experiment which ended quite quickly as a further census taken just six years later in 1884 records none at all. More recently, sheep re-appeared in 1973 but with annual numbers ranging from just 3 to a maximum of 122, this again did not seem very successful and by 1981 they had all gone.

More recently still and contrary to all expectations and accepted local wisdom, sheep were again seen on the Forest in 1990. This time they were not only unexpected but also not particularly welcomed – at least by some. Depastured in the Godshill area they took to raiding gardens and other private property. Fencing proven against ponies and cattle is not necessarily very effective against sheep. This led to some bitter complaints to the Verderers' Court about lack of warning that they were going to be turned out and also the cost of making fences sheep-proof.

The fencing out of stock from private property adjacent to the open forest is one of the very few disadvantages of living in the area. And in this case the responsibility is even more onerous as, if the past is any guide, sheep-proof fencing will only be required for a limited period.

Rights of Fuelwood, Mast and Pasture

Of the remaining three rights all still actively exercised, the common of fuelwood, sometimes known as estovers, assignment wood or sign wood, is probably the most limited. This allows fuelwood to be taken for burning on the fire at home and is unusual in being the only right not exercised exclusively on the open forest. Some years ago the authorities decided that it was inappropriate to plunder the ancient and ornamental woodlands for fuelwood year after year, and it is now cut by the Forestry Commission usually as a by-product of the commercial felling in the inclosures.

The wood for the commoners is cut into four foot lengths and gathered into stacks four feet high by eight feet long, known as cords, and is stored at the ride side with each of the individually numbered cords divided from its neighbour by pieces of upright branch. Towards the end of the summer a letter is sent to each of the commoners with the right, advising them the

Hatchett Pond was originally a series of marl pits.

stack number and location of the cordwood. Being a by-product of the commercial felling which takes place in different parts of the Forest each year, the location of the cordwood in relation to the address of the commoner is purely a matter of chance. In some years it may be quite close by, but in other years the commoner might have to travel to the opposite end of the Forest to collect it.

With the commoners' entitlement ranging from one to as many as ten cords and with each cord weighing around one-and-a-half tons, depending on timber size and length of seasoning, it is a right well worth having particularly as it involves no cost at all other than the effort of collecting it.

Having to do practically all the work themselves and receiving no income at all for it, does not make this the most popular right with the Forestry Commission, or indeed with their predecessors. In the past a good number of these rights, especially those with larger entitlements, have been pur-

chased from the commoners by the Crown and the rights extinguished from the Register. In 1883, a fuelwood return produced by the Office of Woods recorded 130 fuelwood rights receiving 376 cords between them – an average of almost three cords per right – and included ninety-four cords to just seven commoners. By 1983 the number of claimants had been reduced to just under a hundred and the total cordwood to a little over two hundred including just one commoner with an entitlement of ten cords.

Although this undoubtedly represents a great saving in work and effort each year on the part of the Crown, it does seem wrong that it has been allowed to happen. Wrong on the part of the Crown, and equally wrong on the part of the commoner – particularly as the right is attached to a property and the occupier, although able to enjoy the right, is really only holding it in trust for future occupiers.

In some years there is cordwood surplus to the commoners' requirements which is available for sale to the public. For anyone with the facilities

Fuelwood in an inclosure awaiting collection by the commoners.

Stock shading by the Latchmore Brook in high summer.

Right: Pigs at pannage, enjoying the acorns at Denny.

Thousands of stock have been involved in road accidents over the years.

Enjoying the winter sunshine in an otherwise often harsh period.

Nose ringed, ear tagged and full of acorns.

to move and log it, the modest cost makes this an attractive proposition. However with supplies being uncertain, availability needs to be checked with the Forestry Commission at Queen's House with July or August likely to be the best time. Some fallen timber is also available, but contrary to popular belief there is no general right to it. People living within the perambulation and in a property built before 1850 are allowed to pick up twigs and branches from the open forest woodlands provided they do not require cutting and, as the open forest is now car-free, provided a vehicle is not needed either.

On a similar basis and again not a right, it is possible in some parts of the open forest to buy the larger fallen branches and fallen trees from the Commission. Contact with them at Queen's House will result in arrangements being made for the local keeper to meet the prospective purchaser at the tree when the cost will be calculated and the money paid. But there are conditions. The tree must be logged and moved by the end of the month following purchase, safety equipment must be worn if a chainsaw is used and finally, either twenty or forty per cent of the tree – usually the butt end – must be left untouched depending on the area of open forest involved. This last provision is to aid conservation as decaying timber is the basis of the woodland food-chain. Indeed that is why so many large lumps of timber in various stages of decay can be seen around the Forest.

The fifth right is the common of mast which allows pigs to be turned out for sixty days each autumn during the period known as the pannage season. The great advantage of this right is that the pigs will eat the fallen acorns and will positively thrive on them, but if too many are eaten by the other stock without sufficient roughage, they can be poisonous. In years when the acorn crop is heavy, ponies do die from acorn poisoning and periodically when the crop is especially heavy, it is not unknown for fifty or more ponies to die and no doubt this would be even worse but for the pigs.

For very many years the start of the pannage season was fixed at the 25th September quite irrespective of the state of the acorn crop. But nowadays the commencement date is variable and is only announced (at the Verderers' Court) by the Forestry Commission after consultation with the Verderers. Similarly, the actual period of pannage is more flexible than previously. If the acorn crop is very heavy or if, for some reason, not many pigs are turned out, it is not unusual for the season to be extended for a few weeks beyond the normal sixty days. This is normally done at the request of the commoners to allow more time for the pigs to do their work.

Before being turned out all the pigs have to be inspected, nose-ringed and marked – usually with an ear tag – and a small fee also has to be paid. But once on the Forest they will happily spend all day grubbing in the old woods not only putting on weight themselves, but also unknowingly saving undue suffering to the other stock.

The pig numbers vary tremendously from year to year partly reflecting the size of the acorn crop and, to an extent, fluctuations in the market for pork with an overall tendency for numbers to decline in recent decades. During the 1960s there was an average of some 660 turned out each year, peaking at 1,778 turned out in 1962. In the 1970s the yearly average dropped to 240 with a maximum of 969 in 1976. During the 1980s the situation was even worse with the yearly average declining to 185 and a top figure for the decade of just 400 in 1987.

If numbers continue to fall at this rate, the loss of ponies during heavy acorn crop years is going to become unacceptably high and will no doubt lead to increasing numbers of commoners deciding to remove their ponies during this potentially dangerous period. But this will only be a partial answer as without the pigs it will only leave the deer to eat the acorns.

Pigs can be seen on the Forest at times of the year other than the pannage. A number of commons adjacent to the Forest have rights allowing pigs to be turned out at any time and they often wander into the Forest especially in the Bramshaw area. There is also a tradition, rather than a right, that allows a sow with sucking piglets to be turned out at any time provided she is nose-ringed, they do not cause a nuisance and the whole family returns home each evening and does not spend the night on the Forest.

The last and perhaps most familiar of all the rights is the common of pasture or, more properly, the common of pasture of commonable animals.

The old dock in the Verderers' Hall.

This is the right allowing ponies, cattle and donkeys to be depastured on the Forest. Little is known about stock numbers historically, but during the present century there have been some quite major changes with many of these occurring during the first fifty years and being recorded in the Baker Report of 1947.

During the latter part of the nineteenth century total stock on the Forest numbered some 5,500 to 5,700, but by 1915 the total had dropped to 3,200. The situation was slightly reversed during the war years, particularly for cattle, so that by 1920 some 4,550 animals were depastured. The depression years of the 1930s took their toll and by 1940, with just 571 ponies and 908 cattle, the lowest total ever reached was recorded. Once again the war years and the drive for home-grown food resulted in an increase and by 1946, although there were still only 775 ponies, cattle numbers had more than trebled to 3,082. During the next thirty years pony numbers increased rapidly until, in the mid-1970s and with cattle and pony numbers being about equal, the total stock on the Forest exceeded 6,500 being the highest num-

ber recorded during the whole of the century. Since that time the numbers have declined at quite a steady rate with just a hint of a levelling out at about 5,000 to 5,500 by the end of the 1980s.

The potential for accidents is high on the unfenced roads.

The story has been much the same with the donkeys as, throughout the 1939-45 war and during the 1950s and 1960s, they only totalled about a dozen each year on the Forest. Then quite suddenly during the 1970s they became much more popular and within a few years numbers climbed to over a hundred. Since that time numbers have started to fall again and there are now about eighty head to be found.

This story of decline seems to be general with all the stock and although the drop in pony and cattle numbers shows signs of easing, whether or not this is permanent remains to be seen. The number of commoners practising rights has declined from a high in 1976 of 385 down to 303 in 1986 – about the same as the mid-1960s – although here again there are signs that this decline is now easing.

With the mid-1970s having been such an exceptional period for both the total stock depastured and the number of commoners practising their rights, it is difficult to judge if the recent decline is indicative of the future or merely a return to normal after an exceptional peak. But if factors other than figures alone are considered, then the future of commoning in the Forest does not look particularly rosy.

Increasing affluence together with changing financial circumstances both tend to work against commoning. The current ideal of country living is resulting in ever increasing property prices as people retire to the area and others move here and commute to work in Bournemouth, Southampton and even London. These high prices not only tempt existing commoners to sell up and take advantage but make it almost impossible for their children, who have a commoning background, to continue living in the Forest. The situation is being further aggravated as, despite the efforts of the local planning authority, properties are not only being modernised but, more often than not, extended as well and thus further increasing prices. Even land once forming part of commoners' holdings is being sold at prices well beyond normal agricultural value as grazing for riding ponies. With a presumption against much in the way of development in the Forest and no slackening in demand, these ever increasing prices of both land and property seem set to continue.

The number of stock killed and injured on the roads each year works against the commoners as do the poor prices attained for the stock. Even the modifications to the management of the open forest as a result of wildlife interests is thought by some to be affecting the quality of grazing available. With all these various factors and few commoners now having to rely on their rights to provide an essential part of their income, it does result in a very uncertain future for commoning. Indeed the authorities consider this threat so serious that as part of the Management Review undertaken in the late 1980s, they investigated the finances involved in running a 'state' herd of stock on the Forest. But such were the costs involved they concluded that commoning was the only way of ensuring a sufficient level of grazing and browsing to maintain the open and traditional character of the Forest.

The Verderers and the Work of the Court

The control and regulation of the stock rests with the Verderers as it has since 1877 when the Court of Verderers was reconstituted by Parliament. Prior to that date the Verderers were mainly concerned with the administration of the old forest laws and as such, their role eventually became quite limited.

Almost three-quarters of the 1877 Act was devoted to outlining the Verderers' new powers and responsibilities which basically were, and still are, to look after the interests of the commoners and their rights in the New

Forest. Their power to hold the Court of Swainmote and Attachment was retained and they were additionally given powers to employ staff, make byelaws to regulate commoning, to levy fees from the commoners and to enquire into and stop any encroachment or trespass on the open forest.

Previously four in number, the new Court was now to number seven consisting of a chairman or Official Verderer to be appointed by the Crown together with six elected Verderers. To stand for election it was necessary to own, rather than just occupy, at least seventy-five acres of land with some form of common right attaching. To vote in the Verderers' elections it was necessary either to be a registered commoner or to be listed on the electoral role of any parish or town situated entirely or partly within the perambulation.

Although giving a welcome voice to the commoners, with the passage of time this system of elections did become more difficult to operate. The number of people actually owning more than seventy-five acres of land with common rights attaching declined which gave a very limited choice of potential candidates. Whilst the number of potential voters went in the opposite direction and increased dramatically especially after women gained the vote.

Similarly limiting, but this time from the outset, was the financial provision made for the new Court. Authority was given by Parliament for a penny rate to be levied from each property with rights attaching, but this proved unworkable as the cost of collection was found to exceed the income derived. As a result the main income of the Court, then as now, was from marking fees – the fee levied on commoners for each animal depastured. However as stock numbers fluctuate, this income source is very variable and is not at all satisfactory especially as the Court outgoings for staff and the like tend to be constant. Seemingly for as long as the newly reconstituted Court has been in being, there have been periodic complaints about financing difficulties.

The main Court outlay is for the clerk and for the agisters who normally number four. They are employed to supervise the stock on their appointed part of the Forest and it is invariably one or more of the agisters who has to go when Court finances are at a particularly low ebb. Costs of litigation have been a drain on resources, especially in the period following the 1877 Act as the Verderers tried to establish the limit of their powers, and similar costs have been incurred since. At times, the decline in stock numbers and resultant drop in marking fee income has given a balance sheet where outgoings were almost double the income and only two agisters being employed as a result – with each one having to do the work of two men. Even today the problem of Court finance has not been solved.

A further Act of Parliament in 1949 went some way towards solving the electoral and financial problems. The make-up of the Court was increased to ten Verderers, as it remains today, consisting of an Official Verderer appointed by the Crown as previously together with four other appointees; one by the Minister of Agriculture, one by the Forestry Commission, one by Hampshire County Council as the planning authority and one, usually known as the 'amenity' Verderer, appointed by a body concerned with amenity which today is the Countryside Commission. The remaining five Verderers are all elected with qualification to stand being the occupancy, rather than ownership, of at least one acre which has the right of pasture attached. To vote in an election also requires the qualification of occupancy of at least one acre but with any type of right attaching, not necessarily pasture. These alterations considerably widened the choice of candidates whilst restricting the potential voters to those with an active interest in commoning.

This 1949 Act also helped the financial side, but only to a very limited extent and by what can best be described as indirect provision. The responsibility of maintaining the Register of Claims was passed to the Forestry Commission which helped to save both time and money particularly as the information was to be transferred to Ordnance Survey maps. Greater freedom was also given to alter the marking fees which previously had been at a fixed level for very many years, and a new source of income was created from the 'Verderers' Inclosures'. Power was given to the Forestry Commission to inclose up to 5,000 acres for timber cultivation. But this was subject to the Commission first obtaining the Verderers' agreement and paying them compensation for the loss of grazing. In the event only some 2,000 acres was ever inclosed but, to the Court, every bit of income helps. In view of the important role played by the commoners and their stock in the Forest, there does seem to be considerable merit in placing the finances of the Court on a more secure basis and at the very least ensuring that there will always be at least four agisters available to supervise the stock.

The power of the Verderers to stop any encroachment or trespass on the open forest, although welcomed when the threat is from the outside for such things as oil drilling, is not always quite so popular when it directly involves the local population. The saga of the proposed Lyndhurst bypass has now rumbled on since 1925 as a result of the Verderers' decision not to allow it to cross the open forest and opposition by a number of conservation groups. In 1987 Hampshire County Council even promoted a Bill in Parliament seeking to have the Verderers' decision overthrown – but all to no avail. Parliament refused and the Council, or at least the rate-payers, were left with a bill of some tens of thousands of pounds. Whatever the rights or wrongs of a bypass, had Parliament overthrown the Verderers' decision and thus created a precedent, the door would have been opened for any organisation to circumvent the Verderers, and their future powers of protection would have been virtually worthless.

As a result of the bypass problems local opinion has tended to polarise during the late 1980's. Some, who do not want open forest land lost to a bypass, see the Verderers as one of the main guardians of the Forest and as a bastion to outside interference. On the other side and wanting a bypass are many people who consider the Court of Verderers to be an outmoded and undemocratic institution consisting of appointees and Verderers voted into power often by less than four hundred people, and yet holding sway over the whole Forest and its population. But for all these problems, some perceived, others actual, the powers granted by Parliament to the Verderers have, over the years, done far more good than harm.

The Verderers' Hall is attached to the Queen's House in Lyndhurst and this is where the Court sits on the third Monday of alternate months throughout the year. The Hall was originally built in 1388 but greatly modified around 1850, work that was later described by the Deputy Surveyor Gerald Lascelles as 'a destructive alteration as barbarous in character as could be imagined'. Today the Hall does have a certain atmosphere which is helped by some of the fixtures and fittings that survived the change. An ancient canvas with the Royal Arms hangs above the Verderers' bench recording the last visit of the Justice in Eyre in 1669, whilst at the back of the

Hall there is a huge stirrup traditionally believed to have been used for measuring dogs in the early days of forest law, but now known to date from Tudor times. But perhaps most interesting is the dock which, rough hewn with either axe or adze, has every appearance of being of great age, and it is tempting to think that it was once used by offenders against forest law waiting to hear their fate all those centuries ago. Its modern use is rather more prosaic as it is where people stand when making presentments to the Court. This method of presentment allows anyone to take the dock and ask any questions, air any grievance, request action or make any comment concerning commoning and the Forest generally.

When in session, the Court starts at 10.00am with the ten Verderers gathered on the high bench overlooking the Court and is opened by the senior agister with the following words.

> Oyez, Oyez, Oyez. All manner of persons who have any presentment or matter or thing to do at this Court of Verderers, let them come forward and they shall be heard. God save the Queen.

Any announcements or comments are then briefly made by the Official Verderer before the clerk to the Court takes the dock to announce the road accident statistics involving the stock for the previous two months. The Court is then open to hear presentments which may involve just a few people and barely last ten minutes. But if there is a particularly controversial current issue, the number of people and organisations wishing to express an opinion and make their views known can be quite extensive. When everyone has finally had their say, the Court is declared closed by the senior agister and the Verderers retire to continue their discussions in committee.

Thus the Court provides an important avenue for the commoners and public at large to make known their thoughts to the Forest authorities.

The Diverse Life of the Ponies

To the Forest visitor there is little to indicate that common rights are still so widely exercised other than the large number of ponies quietly grazing throughout the area. But their lives are not quite so uneventful as this peaceful activity might suggest.

In the winter, although a number are taken off the Forest, the majority remain with many accompanied by the previous season's foal. Usually they cope very satisfactorily with the feeding difficulties. The latter being towards the end of the winter and particularly in years when there is a late spring. Regular winter inspections, coupled with the power of the agisters to order the removal of any out of condition animals, invariably forestalls any serious difficulties. Although there are differences of opinion as to when a naturally thin pony at the end of the winter is actually out of condition.

Although grazing remains important even during the winter, the ponies do turn to other foodstuffs. Gorse is regularly eaten and is very nutritious despite its prickly nature, and evidence of the amount taken can be seen from the many gorse bushes with a smooth, hedged appearance. Similarly, holly is taken in some quantity and it is this that gives the quite distinct browse

Winter in the Forest – a thick coat and a diet enhanced by gorse and holly.

Pony sales at Beaulieu Road Station are always busy with buyers, sellers and onlookers.

The auctioneer is kept busy as hundreds of ponies change hands.

Agister John Booth tail marking during the annual drift.

Irons in the fire being heated for branding by the agister.

Streamside lawn at Latchmore Bottom, a favourite haunt of the stock.

Although appearing peaceful, the ponies are semi-wild.

line at a height of some five to five and a half feet in many of the old woodlands. Even holly bark is nibbled, often with sufficient fervour to kill part of the tree through ring barking. Fallen trees invariably attract small groups of ponies to eat the twigs. Their enthusiasm for this occasionally resulting in one getting completely caught up in the tangle of branches. Although the decaying timber from the fallen trees is welcomed by the conservationists, this can sometimes prove a mixed blessing for the stock.

Allowing foals to be turned out during their first winter is a source of differing opinions. Some consider that the open forest life is too hard for so young an animal and it should be taken off in the autumn and turned out again in the spring. In contrast, others believe that by allowing a foal to continue to run on the Forest with its dam, it will learn from example how to forage and generally survive and that this will stand it in very good stead for the rest of its life. Whatever the merits of either side, any problems should be picked up by the regular winter inspections or indeed by the commoner who should be keeping a weather-eye on his stock during difficult periods.

Opinions also differ as to the wisdom or otherwise of artificial feeding on the Forest during the winter months. In exceptionally harsh weather some think it is necessary to supplement the natural food available, but others think that this only discourages the ponies from foraging for themselves and, like blue tits in the garden at home, they will simply wait about for the next lot of food to be delivered. If feed is put out, it requires the agreement of the Verderers as to the area and even then there is no guarantee that it will be eaten by the commoner's own stock. It is just as likely that the stock of other commoners will take advantage, as indeed will the deer.

However there is one area of feeding where there is complete agreement; the dangers caused by dumping grass cuttings and other garden waste. Grass cuttings can heat up and other garden waste often contains traces of pesticides, fungicides and other chemicals any of which could cause the death of a pony.

In the summer, there are feeding problems of another sort with some visitors, and even the odd local, giving food to the ponies. This can lead, especially around the car parks where it often happens, to the ponies expecting food and getting upset when they are not given any. Even worse, it can lead to them associating food with vehicles and adding to the already grim toll of road accidents.

The ponies are semi-wild animals, self-sufficient and well able to look after themselves. Giving food, standing directly behind them, getting between a pony and her foal and even, as sometimes seen, placing children on their backs, can lead to accidents. Despite the warning signs, in one three weeks period alone in the late 1980s, Lymington hospital reported treating twenty people – all but one were visitors – for kicks and bites. Left to their own devices the ponies are perfectly harmless, but unthinking involvement is, at the very least, unwise.

For many ponies the only extensive contact they have with man is during the annual drift or round-up which takes place during the autumn. The Forest is divided into some three dozen different areas and the ponies are rounded-up from each in turn with the local agister organising the drift helped by other riders. A number of sweeps are made of the area with bunches of ponies being gathered up and driven back to a temporary holding pen. As expected, a fair degree of horsemanship is required for this as the ponies are on their own home territory which they know intimately and are generally not too keen on being rounded-up. Indeed with many of them having experienced it before, their main aim seems to be to head for the nearest bit of dense gorse or trees.

When as many of the ponies as can be found have been rounded-up, they are taken in small groups to a pound for branding by the agister. Each commoner involved brings his own particular branding iron which, on this occasion, is normally only used for the foals as the older animals will already be carrying a brand. In addition to branding, the agister, when requested by the commoner, will also give a dose of worm mixture to the older animals before tail-marking them. This tail-marking involves cutting the hair on the pony's tail to one of four different shapes depending upon which agister's area is being drifted at the time. It serves as proof that the animal has been rounded-up and recorded and that – ultimately – the commoner has paid the appropriate marking fee for each animal depastured on the Forest.

With the drifts taking place during September, October and usually just into November, it also allows the commoners to decide whether or not to remove any of their stock from the Forest for the winter and saves them the

Ponies are tail marked according to the agister's district.

trouble of having to go out and collect the ponies themselves. To take stock off at other times of the year, they have to do it themselves, and it is usual for commoners to get together for this as it is a job that requires both skill and knowledge.

The final pony sale of the year in the Forest is usually timed to coincide with the final drift of the year and, as a result, is invariably well supported. There are five sales during the year, the first at the end of April or beginning of May, three more during August to October and the last one in November. They are held at Beaulieu Road Station, some two to three miles from Lyndhurst on the Beaulieu road and always on a Thursday. The horse boxes bringing the animals start to arrive from about 8.30am and by 10.30am most of the holding pens are quite full. Five hundred head not being that unusual for the last sale of the year.

The auction gets under way at 10.45am with animals passing through the sales ring at a tremendous rate but sadly, for the last decade or so, not fetching particularly good prices. So low in fact as to allow the meat buyers to bid.

In many ways the sales are reminiscent of a traditional market day with stalls selling anything from hotdogs to clothing and tack and giving many locals the opportunity to meet old friends, complain about the low prices fetched by the ponies and discuss the woes of the world. On a busy day, the great majority of people at the sales are there more for the day out and as interested observers than as active buyers or sellers.

One over-riding area of concern involving the stock and the ponies in particular is the continuing high rate of road accidents. Since the first accident involving a pony and a motor vehicle occurred just after the turn of the century, some thousands have been killed or injured on the Forest roads despite all the efforts over the years to limit the carnage.

At one time almost a third of the stock accidents occurred outside the perambulation, but this was stopped when the perambulation was made stock-proof and all the roads leading in and out of the Forest were gridded by 1963. Even in that year, as the work was being done, there were almost 350 accidents involving over eight per cent of the animals depastured on the Forest. In 1964 the A31 road was fenced and, a few years later, in 1967, the A35 and eventually, by 1975, the A337 Cadnam to Brockenhurst road was finally fenced. All this did help considerably and reduced stock accidents to some two per cent of the animals depastured during the 1970s. But it was not to last as the rate has now risen to about three per cent.

Over the years various ideas have been tried to limit and control the accident rate. In an effort to make the ponies more visible at night when most accidents occur, reflective collars were tried in the 1950's and again in the 1980's, but without any success. A whole array of different road signs have been tried but all have lost their impact within a very few weeks as they just become part of the normal road-side scenery. In the late 1980's a system of experimental raised bars were tried on a road near Sway to reduce traffic speed. Motorists soon discovered that by crossing the bars at speed the severe vibrations would be absorbed by the vehicle's suspension and the exact opposite of the desired effect was achieved.

Now, at the beginning of the final decade of the century and almost one hundred years after the first recorded accident involving a pony, an experimental 40mph speed limit has been introduced in the north of the Forest which, if successful, will be extended to cover the whole area. In addition to the backing of the police, compliance with the new speed limit is also being achieved by the introduction of chicanes or pinch points.

Whether these new limitations will prove to be successful in the long term remains to be seen. If not, the only alternative would be to fence all the Forest roads – work that would not only be expensive but which would largely destroy the open nature of the Forest.

THE PEOPLE'S FOREST

The Rufus Stone in memory of a mysterious death.

Visitors, Pressures and Changes

The New Forest can be described as a people's forest in a number of senses. The tremendous use made of the area for a whole range of leisure and other activities by both visitors and locals alike is perhaps the most familiar aspect. But equally, and some would suggest even more importantly, it is the ability of people to influence both the current management and the future of the area.

With almost three-quarters of the Forest being Crown land which is now vested in the Minister of Agriculture, the area could well be described as a 'state' or 'people's' forest, and as such it is subject to the will and influence of Parliament. In the past, as a result of public pressure, both Parliament and the Minister have brought radical changes to the Forest – something which would have been impossible had the area been entirely in private ownership.

At a more local level most of the management activities undertaken by the Forestry Commission are subject to varying degrees of consultation and, as a result, can be influenced by the public via a range of interested organisations. Even general public opinion has, in the past, built up a sufficient head of steam to induce some quite major changes of course. Membership of the many societies and organisations represented on the Consultative Panel, presentments to the Court of Verderers and now, with the formation of the Heritage Area Committee, representations to both County and District councillors are all avenues of influence available to those who wish to make their voice heard. But perhaps even more than this aspect, it has been the growing leisure use of the Forest since the last war that has really made it a people's forest.

During the last thirty to forty years one of the greatest changes to the

Forest has been the growth of tourism and day visiting together with the growth of all sorts of leisure and recreational activities.

This trend was first noted during the 1950s, and especially during the 1960s, when damage from sheer pressure of numbers started to become apparent. By 1969 there was an estimated three and a half million day visitors and, following the opening of the M27 motorway, the total number of day visitors was calculated at between eight and nine million. The accuracy of this figure is really impossible to confirm as indeed is the statement that it represents a greater usage of the Forest than any other comparably sized area in the country. But certainly the use of the area is great and continues to grow year by year.

Until comparatively recently the majority of visitors came during high summer, but gradually the season extended until now, even in winter if the weather is fine and sunny, the weekends can be almost as busy as the summer. For all these large numbers and traffic often stretching back from Lyndhurst to Cadnam and the M27, it is still possible, even during the busiest Bank Holiday, to walk the Forest and hardly see a soul.

But these increasing pressures did bring change, particularly during the early 1970s. The indiscriminate use of the open forest by vehicles and campers was stopped and the whole area made car-free, and a network of some 140 car parks was developed providing spaces for about five thousand vehicles. Regular monitoring of the vehicle use in the Forest generally and the car parks in particular during the past twenty years has resulted in little or no alterations being required which does say quite a lot for the original choice of sites.

The other main change was the provision of a number of caravan sites in addition to the existing sites at Hollands Wood and Holmsley and the prohibition of over-night or wild camping in the Forest other than on the sites provided. Before this alteration, which was not welcomed by some of the regular campers, the restrictions on camping were few and far between. Camping was not allowed in Queen's Bower or Mark Ash or within a hundred yards of an inclosure fence or, indeed, within two hundred yards of a house unless it was occupied by a forest keeper or forester. With many of the keepers – or more likely their wives – also being responsible for issuing camping permits, they at least were doubtless happy to see the changes taking place.

Once settled in the Forest, the only other limitation for the camper was the requirement to dig a hole at least twelve inches deep to use as a latrine together with a second hole of similar depth for the disposal of 'foul water'. If litter bins were not available nearby, then yet a further hole at least twelve inches deep had to be dug for rubbish. Although all of these holes were covered up before the camper left the area, with over 650,000 camper nights (one camper staying for one night) in 1970 alone, it was obvious that some change was necessary, quite apart from the erosion and other damage being caused by the heavy use of some of the more popular areas.

Despite some complaints by regular campers, the additional caravan sites were readily accepted as the most viable alternative and their use rapidly accelerated until, by 1980, there was some 850,000 camper nights and the sites were operating to near capacity. So great was their popularity that during one memorable Spring Bank Holiday weekend, with all the pitches occupied early, prospective campers still kept arriving. This resulted in the

Camping and caravanning is now restricted to the camp sites.

Forest being brought to a virtual standstill and the police directing campers straight through the Forest vaguely in the direction of Bournemouth and the west country. This hard lesson gave rise to a system of pre-booking for this particular period and, for a number of years, twenty-four hours a day wardening of all the sites, even the informal ones, for the bulk of the holiday weekend.

Today, the twelve sites together with the overflow areas give a capacity of some 5,200 pitches. However, following declining use during the early 1980's there have been suggestions made by the Management Review Group that one site be closed and that the use of others be modified. But since that time, as the situation has reversed and the use of the sites is increasing again, precipitate action would not seem wise.

The large sites at Ashurst, Holland's Wood and Holmsley are all fully equipped and provide some forty per cent of the pitches, whilst the semi-equipped sites at Longbeech, Ocknell and Roundhill provide some thirty-five per cent. The remaining sites are all informal and provide only minimum facilities. Despite complaints still occasionally heard that the camp sites take valuable grazing, most are open to the stock and the majority close at the end of September with Ashurst remaining open until the end of October and just Setthorns being open throughout the year. Having the benefit of electrical hook-ups, Setthorns is popular during the winter and even at Christmas is often quite full. Thanks to the various authorities concerned with the alterations during the 1970's, the sites are well screened, sympathetically situated and in a variety of areas making them as popular with the holidaymakers as they are unnoticed by the locals.

Lyndhurst High Street, the often too busy capital of the Forest.

Lyndhurst church spire seen from Matley Heath. It is a landmark for miles around.

Boldre church near Lymington, dating from the thirteenth century.

The fox hound meet at Lucy Hill, pursuing a long tradition of hunting in the Forest.

Lymington River at Balmer Lawn, a summer favourite with the children.

In many ways it seems almost incongruous to talk about the Forest's attractions being mainly the peace, quiet and unspoilt nature and, at the same time, to talk of visitor numbers by the millions. But the attractions of the Forest are largely low-key with great efforts being made by the authorities to retain the traditional nature and feel of the area. The comparatively large size helps to absorb the numbers and, with the bulk of the Forest being Crown land, the Forestry Commission are able to exercise fairly rigorous control.

The byelaws governing the use of the Forest are very comprehensive and consist of what can best be described as common sense limitations designed to protect the area and its peaceful enjoyment. In most cases the mere fact that byelaws are in force is sufficient deterrent and prosecutions are almost unknown. Although in some cases, such as allowing dogs to run out of control and worry the stock and deer, the odd well-publicised prosecution would perhaps not go amiss.

Street trading is not allowed on the open forest although ice-cream vans will be seen, but only in certain areas and all of them only as a result of successfully tendering for the exclusive use of an area for the season. The various signs required are kept to a minimum and are of a discreet design. The many potential group activities are controlled with some, such as various types of motor sport, not being allowed as they are out of keeping with the Forest. But for all the control which, it must be said, many people do not realise exists anyway, there is lots to see both in and around the Forest.

The Villages and Towns

Aptly known as the capital of the Forest, Lyndhurst is a busy centre where a number of main roads meet resulting in a weight of traffic – especially during the summer – being out of all proportion to its modest size of some 3,000 people. Many of the authorities concerned with the management of the Forest are based here. The offices of both the District Council and the Nature Conservancy Council are to be found either side the grassy expanse of Bolton's Bench, whilst at the top of the High Street, beyond the church, is the oldest building in the village, Queen's House. Although dating mainly from the seventeenth century, parts are far older and include both Tudor and medieval remains. Originally used as lodgings by the King when hunting in the area and later as a residence by the Crown's chief representative, after a period of being privately rented it is now the administrative centre for the Forestry Commission in the New Forest. With quite extensive grounds behind contrasting with the hustle and bustle of the village, it is easy to visualise how peaceful and sleepy Lyndhurst must have been at one time.

The Verderer's Court is attached to the eastern end of Queen's House but sadly is not open to the public other than when the Court is in session every second month.

In the centre of the village next to the car park is the newly opened Museum and Visitor Centre which was developed as part of the Forest's 900th anniversary celebrations. Among the many imaginative displays is the

New Forest Embroidery which was commissioned by the New Forest Association and designed by Belinda Montagu also as part of the anniversary celebrations. Telling the story of the New Forest and its wildlife, the embroidery was originally designed in three sections totalling twenty-five feet in length to hang on the wall between the windows of the Verderer's Court.

Yachts at Lymington are even more numerous during carnival week.

In addition to the Museum, the building also houses an Educational Trust which, among many other things, organises walks and talks on various aspects of the Forest for both visitors and locals. The Tourist Information Centre also has a permanent home in the same complex.

Overlooking the village the tall spire of the Victorian church provides a landmark for miles around and, in the churchyard, a childhood memory for many. Here will be found the grave of Mrs Reginald Hargreaves who, as Miss Alice Liddell, was best known for her starring role in Lewis Carroll's imaginative childrens' stories.

The churches in the area generally are interesting and many are worth a visit. Just a couple of miles from Lyndhurst at Minstead the rather mixed architecture of the very old church is as attractive as the inside is interesting – particularly for the unusual three-decker pulpit. Traditionally the lower deck was used by the Parish Clerk to say the 'amens', the middle deck for reading the scriptures and the top deck for preaching the sermon. With a font dating from Norman times or perhaps earlier, a gallery and, in the churchyard, the grave of another well known literary figure, Arthur Conan Doyle, it is an engaging place.

At Brockenhurst, an ancient village which has developed largely as a result of the main line railway station, the church lies outside the village and, like so many of the others, is built on a hill. Again the architecture is quite mixed with a Norman nave, thirteenth century chancel and eighteenth century brick tower. At the entrance to the church is a yew reputedly – as so many of them tend to be – a thousand years old. The village centre is rather less geared to tourism than most but in common with the other villages, with the exception of Lyndhurst, is open to the rather dubious pleasures of the wandering stock, especially donkeys.

In the north of the Forest Bramshaw church and, in the south, although strictly outside the perambulation, Boldre church both have their own special interest, whilst at Beaulieu there are the impressive remains of the once thriving Cistercian monastery. This was established on land originally given by King John in 1204 and developed into a rich and powerful centre until being dissolved in 1538 and sold to the Earl of Southampton. Today the National Motor Museum and other attractions make Beaulieu one of the leading tourist centres in the whole country visited by tens of thousands each year, although few spare but a passing glance at the abbey ruins nearby.

Further south on the Beaulieu Estate, the great barn at Saint Leonards, reputed once to have been the largest in Europe, provides ample evidence of the success of the monks, whilst just a mile away on the Beaulieu River at Buckler's Hard there is evidence of failure – although not by the monks.

During the early 1700s the 2nd Duke of Montagu developed Montagu Town (now Buckler's Hard) intending it to be a free port for the import of sugar from his new estates in the West Indies and presumably to avoid the necessity of paying port dues elsewhere. Unfortunately, as a result of problems with his new estates the venture failed and it was almost twenty years before it was finally rented out and used for shipbuilding. During the following seventy years many wooden war ships, including the *Agememnon* and the 74-gun *Illustrious*, were built at the yard although not, as is so often assumed, using timber from the New Forest. Timber from the Royal forest went to Royal ship yards; the timber used by private yards came from private sources.

With planning being such a sensitive issue, it is unlikely than an enterprise as large as Beaulieu would ever have been allowed to develop today. Indeed, current policy is to site such attractions outside the Forest to ease the pressure of visitors. In consequence, more recent developments such as the Butterfly Farm at Ashurst and Paulton's Park at Ower, both of which attract many thousands of visitors, are outside the perambulation. One disadvantage of these so called honeypots being all around is that although they do attract many people away from the Forest, they also tend to make the Forest area generally an even better centre for the holidaymaker by providing such a wide range of interests.

Just outside, although spiritually part of the Forest, Lymington, with its

attractive water-front setting is a popular yachting centre and busy market town. To the west of the Forest, Fordingbridge, and a few miles down the River Avon, Ringwood, are both ancient towns with their own particular personality and interest.

With the cathedral cities of Salisbury and Winchester both only half an hour or so from the Forest by car, and the seaside attractions of Bournemouth a similar distance to the west and Southampton and Portsmouth to the east, the New Forest is at the centre of a great range of interests.

The remains of Beaulieu Abbey, a quiet corner of a popular attraction.

Information signs add to the interest of the waymarked walks.

The Reptiliary, Deer Sanctuary and Forest Interpretation

In the Forest itself, the facilities are essentially limited and primarily involve the wildlife and the natural scene. The complex of half a dozen fields that make up the Boldrewood Deer Sanctuary is one of the most popular areas. Since the very severe winter of 1963, food has been placed in the fields every day other than during the autumn rutting season and a few weeks after. Over the years, although they are free to come and go as they please, the fallow deer have found the fields to be a safe haven and can be seen at most times of the year. Although when the keeper brings the food in the middle of the afternoon they respond to his calls, the deer do remain nervously alert and will quickly move away if there is too much noise or disturbance from the two observation platforms provided at the edge of the fields. For those able to visit the sanctuary regularly, it is an ideal place to see the deer change throughout the year. The casting of the antlers by the bucks in early spring and the gradual regrowth during the summer. A little later in the spring, the change of coat colour to the paler, spotted summer coat and again in the autumn back to the subdued winter colouring. But perhaps most attractive of all is the does bringing in their new-born fawns from the end of June when, with some good fortune, it is possible to see as many as a couple of dozen playing together.

Other facilities provided by the Commission are the wildlife observation hides at Frame Heath Inclosure and Queen's Meadow. These hides, mainly advertised to holidaymakers and, as a result, little-known to locals, can be hired from the Forestry Commission at Queen's House at modest cost. The raised hide at Frame Heath Inclosure is in the middle of an area not generally available to the public because of deer research and overlooks an area where sika deer are often to be seen. At Queen's Meadow (situated along the south side of Hursthill Inclosure), fallow deer often congregate in large numbers sometimes with a few red deer in with them. Although they can be seen quite easily over the fence surrounding the field, the raised hide does give a more panoramic view. One side advantage is that the enforced stillness of being in a hide often results in far more wildlife being seen than just deer alone.

Wildlife of another and somewhat less popular type can be found at Holidays Hill, some two miles from Lyndhurst on the A35 Christchurch road. Here is the reptiliary where, in a series of compounds, examples of all the reptiles and amphibians found in the Forest can be seen. With such rare and elusive creatures as the smooth snake and sand lizard this is probably the best place to see them, but even in such a comparatively restricted space, they can be surprisingly difficult to spot and it takes little imagination to appreciate the difficulties of seeing them in the wild.

At both Brockenhurst and Burley horse drawn wagon or wagonette rides are available which provide a pleasurable hour or so seeing some of the Forest at a pace more common a hundred years ago. For the rather more energetic, there are a series of waymarked walks mainly found along the Rhinefield and Boldrewood Drive, the small road that runs north from the west of Brockenhurst, across the A35 road and up to the Deer Sanctuary. All the walks have attractive leaflets available from dispensers and with the

The Reptiliary at Holidays Hill is best visited on a warm sunny day.

various information plaques along the route, these highlight the points of interest.

The Ober Water walks start from Whitefield Moor car park next to the extensive lawn just to the west of Brockenhurst. Even the longest of the two walks only takes some sixty minutes and follows the attractive Ober Water stream, the haunt of grey wagtails and the odd kingfisher. If time is available, it is possible to follow the path downstream beyond the marked walk to the Aldridgehill caravan site then, crossing the bridge to the right-hand side of the stream, down to Bolderford Bridge and the Lymington River. Although

a large scale (1:25000) Ordnance Survey map is advisable to save getting lost, the Lymington River can be followed upstream through Queen's Bower and on to Queen's Meadow, the site of the wildlife hide. The return can either be by retracing the route or by heading due south across the heathland to the caravan site and then up the Ober Water to the waymarked walk again.

A little higher up the Rhinefield Drive, past Rhinefield House, the Black-water car park and, still further, the Brock Hill car park, both have short waymarked walks together with a rather longer walk linking the two parks. This aptly named Tall Trees walk between the two car parks contains many fine conifer specimens including a pair of Wellingtonias each well over one

A peaceful days fishing on Cadman's Pool.

hundred and fifty feet high. From Brock Hill there is a short walk through one of the timber inclosures, whilst from the Blackwater car park the walk follows the Blackwater stream for a short distance and then through the developing arboretum. This whole area is surrounded by inclosures where a range of both broadleaf and conifer species will be found growing. With both grass and gravel rides the walking is easy but with so many of them looking alike, loosing a sense of direction is similarly easy.

Continuing further north, across the A35 road and to the top of Boldrewood Drive is the Boldrewood car park, the centre for another series of walks and the Deer Sanctuary. In following the various walks it is hard to believe that many of them were completely blocked following the storm of January 1990 or indeed that the Boldrewood Drive itself was blocked for much of its length. Although many fine trees remain to be admired in the Arboretum, a good number were lost and much of the damage is still in evidence. Fortunately the Radnor Stone, the memorial to the Earl of Radnor who was chairman of the Forestry Commission and later the Official Verderer, escaped the storm unscathed. Set in a quiet corner, it has a charming series of engravings depicting the wildlife of the Forest.

The last waymarked walk is at Wilverley Inclosure in the south-west of the Forest, an area almost entirely devoted to conifer. Alongside the inclosure is the wide, grassy expanse of Wilverley Plain which is greatly favoured by the stock whilst nearby, there are the weather-bleached remains of the Naked Man. Although little remains of this old oak now, it is reputed to have been used as a hanging tree for smugglers caught in the act and stood beside a road which once passed along this edge of the inclosure. The heathland in this area has lots of interest including butterfly orchids and the rare wild gladiolus and, later in the year, wonderful displays of the field gentian. But perhaps the best time of all to visit is in late August when the heather is in full bloom and the air is alive with buzzing insects and shimmering heat.

Another way of exploring the Forest is to take advantage of the many guided walks available. In the past the Forestry Commission has organised a series of walks from both the main camp sites and from Bolton's Bench in Lyndhurst, whilst the Educational Trust at the Museum has organised a further series leaving from selected car parks. But from 1990 this was rationalised and there are now over a hundred guided walks available during the summer leaving variously from the camp sites and Bolton's Bench. At some one and a half to two hours duration and at minimal cost, these will no doubt prove as popular as the previous series.

Coupled with weekly slide shows at the Museum during the summer, this trend towards explaining the working of the Forest and its wildlife will probably expand over the years as an effective way of promoting awareness and greater appreciation of the area.

Hunting, Fishing and other Activities

In addition to the day-visitors and holidaymakers, the Forest is also extensively used by the locals and people from the immediate surrounding areas for a great range of purposes, some of which are becoming increasing-

ly controversial. The reason for some of this controversy is partly changing attitudes and also, in every likelihood, the changing make-up of the Forest population which contains ever increasing numbers of incomers and retired people who may have a more idealised view of the area.

With the flowering of the heather in August comes the bee hives.

Hunting still continues as it has for the last nine hundred years, although these days often needing the presence of both the police and keepers to ensure peace between the huntsmen and the anti-hunting and animal rights lobby. During the winter months hunting takes place on five, and sometimes, six days of the week with specific days being allocated to each of the three hunts which are permitted under licence from the Forestry Commission.

The buck hounds are out each Monday and Friday after fallow buck and these days they are the only pack in the country involved with this species. The number of bucks taken each season is but a tiny fraction of those culled by the Forest keepers to control numbers, and it is this sporting rather than any sort of control activity that fuels the controversy. But, as is so often said about the buck hounds, were it not for deer hunting there would probably not be a New Forest.

Tuesdays, Saturdays and the occasional Thursday are for the fox hounds which, each year, account for about twenty per cent of the total estimated local fox population. Although in some areas of the country fox hunting is the best, and in some cases the only method of fox control, in an area like the New Forest where the ground is so extensively keepered, it is the sporting rather than control aspect that again causes concern to many.

The beagle pack that hunts the hare is probably the least-known, but it also is the source of some concern – but of a rather different nature. Hunting on both Wednesdays and Saturdays, though spending a number of days off the Forest, its quarry, the brown hare, is apparently declining in the Forest and doubts have been expressed about its future. The recent Management Review recommended that hunting be allowed to continue, despite requests for a temporary ban, but that a survey of the status of the hare in the Forest be undertaken by the Nature Conservancy Council. In such a difficult area and with the hare population being comparatively low, this will no doubt take some years to complete.

Strong and contrasting passions also arise, although on a considerably lesser scale, from model aircraft flying in the forest. This has taken place for a number of years on one small part of the old airfield area at Beaulieu Heath and has long produced spasmodic complaints of excessive noise and of the users venturing outside the designated area causing disturbance to the wildlife. A suggestion was made in the Management Review that it be stopped. But such was the campaign organised by the club with representations being made both locally and from around the country including some from Members of Parliament, that the activity was allowed to continue with the proviso that a more suitable alternative venue be found if possible. Although certainly noisy and rather intrusive, the flying appears to have little effect on the wildlife in the area where recently at least one pair of dartford warblers was seen nesting alongside the flying area.

Duke of Edinburgh Award Scheme activities pass largely unremarked but the orienteering events do produce complaints of disturbance. Similarly, concern is being expressed about the path and track erosion in the area of some of the riding schools where continual daily use is the cause of a dilemma. By its very nature, there are only a limited number of routes available from the various riding schools and short of providing special gravel tracks to protect the natural fabric, the problem is very difficult to solve. To date no solutions have been offered other than to prohibit the development of further riding schools within the perambulation.

Not all of the many activities and uses of the Forest are controversial. When the heather is in bloom, bee hives appear throughout the heathland areas with their siting carefully controlled by the Forestry Commission. With some five to six hundred hives being out in a normal year and many people not being at all happy having to walk too close to them, not only are the number of hives in a given area controlled, but also the direction of the hive entrance. Bee-keeping is a traditional activity and evidence from long ago can still be seen around the Forest. Small banked inclosures have been found where it is thought hives were once kept protected from the stock. These small 'bee gardens' as they have been called are assumed to have resulted in some Forest place names such as Hive Garn Bottom near Pitts Wood and one or two others.

Fishing also takes place, although trout fishing on the streams is no longer allowed. Course fishing is available at Hatchett Pond and Cadman's Pool with fishing permits being available from a variety of centres in and around the Forest. The children are not forgotten as they are allowed to fish to their hearts content free of charge at both Janesmoor and Roundhill Ponds.

The Forest is extensively used as a huge open air laboratory and study centre. Visitors from abroad come to see the forestry practised and how the great diversity of uses blend one with another. School children make extensive use of the area and this has been helped – and extended – by the Educational Trust based at the Museum in Lyndhurst. But perhaps most of all it is the wildlife and habitats that are studied and with such a diversity of both, the Forest makes an ideal centre.

Studies are undertaken by individuals pursuing a variety of personal interests; by various local natural history societies and by universities whose students are studying everything from the life of the ticks to the behaviour of the deer. Apart from the greater understanding and knowledge gained, all this information helps the Forestry Commission to formulate their management policies and avoid unknowingly causing damage to the flora and fauna.

With all the dog-walking, kite-flying and myriad other uses made of the Forest, it is not only surprising that they should all blend together but that the area should still support such a wealth of wildlife.

Walking, the best way to see the area

Of all the various activities, the most popular by far is walking which is enjoyed by both visitors and locals. Whether used for just a gentle stroll or a more serious walk complete with day pack, the Forest has many advantages. The walking is essentially easy and although an Ordnance Survey map is advisable, the chances of getting seriously lost are few. In fact it is impossible to be more than two miles away from any of the Forest roads. Unlike hill walking, the weather is rarely a problem but with the large number of bogs a certain amount of planning is sometimes needed if annoying detours are to be avoided. Indeed such is the amount of boggy land about, and streams, that other than during the summer season a pair of 'Wellingtons' will often allow greater freedom of movement than walking boots. But perhaps the biggest problem in such a large area is where to go to see the true Forest and obtain some peace and quiet away from the more popular areas.

Among the more attractive features are the Forest streams which meander through a whole range of Forest scenery. In the north, the Latchmore stream rises in Islands Thorns Inclosure and runs through the largely broadleaf inclosures of Amberwood and Alderhill before reaching the open heath at Latchmore Bottom. During early May bluebells are a feature of these woodlands, whilst in high summer Latchmore Bottom is the site of a large shade where, during spells of hot weather, stock often gather in quite

The ever changing scene makes walking very attractive.

The Ober Water, one of a
number of streams well worth
exploring.

large numbers to stand out the heat of the day before moving off at night to feed.

The central section of the larger Lymington River between Millyford and Balmer Lawn near Brockenhurst runs mainly through ancient and ornamental woodland and is particularly pretty in the spring as the new leaves break and again in the autumn with the turning colour. The meandering stream with its alternating shallows and deeper pools is ideal for kingfishers and grey wagtails, whilst in the surrounding ancient woods, deer and all the typical woodland birds will often be seen. The wealth of fallen and decaying timber is typical of many of the old woodland areas and with the odd grazing pony gives a timeless feel.

In contrast, the Beaulieu River, although sometimes tree-lined, runs mainly across heathland and streamside lawns such as Longwater. Because of the wet ground it can be difficult to approach in some areas and, also for this reason, difficult to walk its whole length. But with wading birds breeding on the boggy areas in the spring, damselflies and dragonflies around the stream during the summer and, rather later, the rare marsh gentian found on some of the wet, sloping ground, it is a stream well worth exploring.

In an attempt to drive to the quieter places, the areas flanking the main roads are often ignored sometimes because the road side fencing is thought to indicate private land rather than is actually the case, to keep the stock off the road. Although initially noisy, once a few hundred yards away from the road the peace gradually returns and more often than not you are on your own. Just to the north of the A31 road the series of heathland valleys running from King's Garden to Handy Cross Plain and passing the edge of Roe and Pinnick Woods, are well worth exploring, whilst to the south of the main road the sweet chestnut dominated Backley Inclosure and nearby Bratley Wood with its lovely old beeches, is similarly worth a look. Even some of the place names in this area such as Harvest Slade Bottom, Stinking Edge and Mouse's Cupboard are enough to tempt exploration if only for the sake of curiosity.

Towards the Cadnam end of the A31, and again to the north, at Canterton, the curious might also be drawn to see the Rufus Stone. This cast-iron monument enclosing an earlier stone memorial is said to mark the spot where King William II, better known as Rufus, was shot by an arrow in August 1100. Although shot by Sir Walter Tyrrell, whether by accident or design remains a mystery. And as the original stone memorial was not erected until 1745, some six hundred and fifty years after the event, even its placement is in doubt.

The pollarded, four-hundred years old Knightwood Oak near the A35 road is a must for a Forest visitor, whilst about a mile away the far less well known – and less impressive – Eagle Oak is reputed to be where the last white-tailed eagle in the Forest was shot in 1810. All of the surrounding areas here are down to inclosures with many, such as Knightwood Inclosure, giving a good idea of the range of species and ages grown for timber which is in sharp contrast to the even-aged monoculture often practised in other parts of the country.

Further down the A35 road Markway Bridge crosses the Mill Lawn Stream which is another attractive walking area. To the east behind Markway Inclosure the undulating heathland around Duck Hole Bottom and Wilverley is a picture when the heather is in bloom. To the west, the scattered trees and lawns around Redrise Hill and Mill Lawn have their own particular character.

For the walker the great joy of the Forest is that no two areas are the same. The ancient woodlands of Tantany and Honey Hill near Pig Bush have a totally different feel to Eyeworth Wood near Fritham which itself is different from Ridley Wood near Picket Post. Similarly the almost rugged heathland of Vales Moor in the west is in contrast to the flat expanse of Beaulieu Heath with its old airfield and unexpected variety of wildlife. Indeed the only way to get to know the Forest is to walk and to explore the many areas that have seemingly changed little since the days of William.

A pleasurable way of seeing the early August heather near Wilverley.

The stream at Holidays Hill, as the grey wagtails and kingfishers never see it.

Beauty and peace in the dead of winter, near Pound Hill.

THE WILD FOREST

Badger, the reward for quiet and patient watching.

The Making of the Habitats

The unique development of the Forest over the centuries coupled with the natural advantages of situation, soil and climate have together produced a great diversity of habitats supporting a range of wildlife considered by many to be among the very best in the country.

Sitting on a downfold of chalk variously infilled with sands and clays and, in many areas, topped with a layer of gravel, the Forest soil tends to be poor though quite variable. The best of the soils are generally to be found in the south of the area which has resulted not only in the main development of villages and smallholdings, but also the best of the wildlife interest. The southerly slope of the Forest from a high point of just over four hundred feet at Telegraph Post down to sea level at the Solent also tends to favour the southern half. In consequence, to the north of the mainly wooded central area it is more sparsely populated and has fewer roads and generally has a more open and almost rugged appearance with rolling heathland and steep sided valleys more reminiscent of high moorland, than the softer landscape in the south of the Forest.

The mild, dry weather plays an important role in ensuring that such rare creatures as the sand lizard, smooth snake and Dartford warbler are able to survive throughout the year. In this, the Forest's central position on the south coast is of great advantage. Falling midway between the mild, wet Atlantic influenced climate to the west and the dry though colder continental climate to the east coupled with its position in the extreme south and low altitude, produces a climate which is both mild and generally lacking extremes. As a result, the summers are warm with an average maximum temperature of 21C, whilst even more importantly, the winters are mild with average temperatures ranging between a minimum of 1C and a maximum of

7C. The total rainfall is only just over 30" (76.5cm) a year and is very evenly spread. From February to July the average is about 2" (5.1cm) a month and this rises to around 3" (7.6cm) a month for the rest of the year.

Heathland near Deadman Hill, a nationally important habitat.

But for all the benefits of a mild, dry climate and soil conditions that were largely impossible for agriculture for many centuries, the greatest influence on the area has probably been the many and varied activities of man.

Starting some five thousand years ago the partial clearance of virgin woodland for agriculture by the Bronze Age and earlier peoples is thought to have resulted in the impoverishment of the soils and development of the heathland. The subsequent development of commoning with the widespread exploitation of the soil and extensive grazing of stock – not to mention the grazing and browsing activities of the deer – has helped to maintain the open appearance of the area and greatly influenced the plant life. In more recent times the active physical management, following the decline of the commoner's exploitation, has become increasingly geared to wildlife considerations and the need to protect the biological diversity. And it is this very diversity that is the key to the wealth of wildlife.

The jewel in the Forest's crown is the 48,000 acres of open forest which consists almost entirely of habitats – such as heath, ancient woodland and bogs – that are either becoming increasingly rare elsewhere or have disappeared altogether.

The dominant Forest habitat is the heathland which, covering some 30,000 acres, is now the largest complex left in the country, said to be the largest in Europe, and, as such, is of international importance. Elsewhere in Hampshire, and in Surrey, many of the heathland areas have now gone, whilst in Dorset, the heathland county and made famous by Hardy, the change has been dramatic. Partly as a result of conversion for agriculture, but mainly for building development to meet the demands of an increasing population, the heathland that once covered well over 100,000 acres of the county has now been reduced to less than 15,000 acres according to a recent survey.

The ancient and ornamental woodland in the Forest which, being open to the stock, should more properly be referred to as pasture woodland, covers some 8,000 acres. As pasture woodland this again is said to be the largest complex left in the country. Elsewhere it is the same old story of destruction. Many old woodlands have either been clear felled or converted to conifer and as a result, many counties have lost up to half their old woodlands whilst at least one has lost over two-thirds.

Finally with these main habitats, there are the valley bogs covering some 7,000 acres, an area said to be greater than all of the bogs put together in the rest of England. Although not the most popular, these areas are important and many have a far greater range of interest, particularly plants, than a brief glance would indicate. The other wet areas include streams which total well over one hundred miles in length together with a large range of ponds varying in both size and acidity. Some of the ponds occur naturally, but many are of artificial origin. Sometimes disconcerting to the walker are the bogs, known as flushes, that are to be found on many hillsides. These are to be found where the water readily seeps through the gravel capping of the hill and, on meeting the impervious material below, seep out through the hillside, creating bogs that often have their own particular interest.

The wide range of wildlife associated with these unusual habitats results partly from their sheer size and partly because of the diversity that occurs in them. Heathland varies from damp to dry, some of it supports gorse whilst bracken occurs in other areas and also lawn and stands of self-sown pine. Similarly, the old woodlands can range from having a thick, almost gloomy undercover of holly to being very open with scattered glades where fallen trees have allowed more light to filter through the canopy. In some areas beech are dominant and oak in others, whilst even the amount of dead and decaying timber and the strength or otherwise of the natural regeneration results in one woodland never being quite the same as another. The bogs also vary in age, size and interest with many of them having an unbroken

history of 7,000 years or more and some have a peat depth up to twenty feet.

Although these areas are the best-known and most treasured of the Forest habitats, other areas are important and help to add to the overall interest. The 12,000 or so acres of conifers in the inclosures provide a home for a number of creatures that might not otherwise occur and the 8,000 acres of broadleaf add yet further to the variety, but with the best of the interest generally being where the inclosures are fully fenced. Even the privately owned land provides a network of fields and hedgerows which is of value to the less specialised flora and fauna.

In addition to the variety of habitat, it is the intermingling and gradual blending of one with another that results in such a rich mosaic which is as much a delight to the eye as it is valuable for the wildlife.

Snow at Eyeworth Pond, a rare sight in the Forest.

Adders although quite common are not often seen.

Amphibians, Lizards and Snakes

Five of our six native amphibians are to be found in the Forest with the status of all of them being reasonably secure – certainly when compared to the situation found elsewhere in the country.

Common frogs use a wide range of ponds and even large temporary puddles and although breeding normally occurs during February, during the recent spell of mild winters spawning has been taking place in January and sometimes even during late December. As a result, they tend to be more widespread than concentrated, but in one small, unnamed pond near Burley accumulations of over a thousand have been recorded.

In contrast, common toads which usually breed some two to three weeks later than the frogs in the Forest, appear to be much more selective in their breeding waters probably because they are less willing to accept such a wide range of water acidity. Concentrations of up to a thousand do occur with one pond, again unnamed and near Burley, being particularly impressive. But with toads especially, watching after dark with the aid of a torch can often give a better idea of numbers than during the hours of daylight, though care is needed – for the sake of the toads rather than the count – as it is not unusual for a number to be sitting on the pond banks.

Despite periodic reports over the years, the natterjack toad remains the only native amphibian missing from the Forest and in many ways it is surprising that they should have died out as a number of areas do seem most suitable for them. A similar fate also seems to be facing the once well known colony of tree frogs near Beaulieu which has now all but gone. These tiny green frogs that once inhabited a bamboo thicket and pond nearby in quite good numbers used to provide an unusual background chorus during mild May evenings for the patrons of the pub close by – but sadly no longer.

The other three amphibians are all newts which are not the easiest of creatures to see other than perhaps during the breeding season. The palmate newt appears to be the most widespread as, like the frog, they are more tolerant of acid water. Smooth newts are found rather less frequently, whilst the nationally rare great crested newt is limited in just a handful of areas. All the newts return to the breeding ponds in early spring and they are probably best seen after dark from March to May when they are often to be found on the surface.

Unlike the chilly weather and inconvenient times often associated with seeing amphibians, reptiles prefer the warm, sunny days of summer. Both snakes and lizards start to emerge from hibernation from about mid-March and during this early part of the season can often be seen basking during sunny weather, sometimes for the greater part of the day. As the season develops and the temperatures gradually rise, they become more active and are then perhaps best seen during the first three hours of daylight in the morning or the last couple of hours in the evening.

The aptly named common lizard is found throughout much of the heathland and other areas including gardens. More often than not, the only indication of their presence is a quick rustle in the heather as they are disturbed, but with five or ten minutes patient waiting they will invariably make a cautious reappearance. Similarly common though far more elusive, the slowworm tends to be rather secretive and has a general preference for damp, shady places. This attractive bronze coloured legless lizard can be encountered by chance almost anywhere on the damper heathland, woodland and gardens, especially where there is a rockery or some dry stone walling.

In comparison to the other two lizards, the sand lizard, a nationally rare species, is becoming increasingly unusual in the Forest with its numbers being largely maintained by captive-bred stock. The reason for the decline is uncertain as the preferred habitat of dry, sandy, undulating heath with south facing slopes for basking and clear area of sandy soil for egg-laying do occur in the Forest in reasonable quantity. The missing factor appears to be mature, open heather which they require for hunting their insect prey. This is generally lacking in the Forest due to the policy of heathland management,

Male sand lizard, an increasingly rare species in the Forest.

and particularly burning. The high rate of predation, although not confined to the Forest, is another factor with both fully grown and especially juveniles being taken by a variety of predators. Captive breeding does control the very high rate of juvenile mortality, but whether it will ever result in active and sufficiently large self-maintaining colonies remains to be seen.

In addition to the three native lizards, all three native snake species are to be found in the Forest including the only poisonous species, the adder which is often a cause for concern among many people. Even in this supposedly enlightened age it is still common practice in some areas to automatically kill a snake on sight irrespective of whether it is an adder, a harmless grass snake or the very rare smooth snake. All too often it is

Old woodpecker holes are ideal for the grey squirrels.

Marsh gentians, now rare elsewhere but still found around many of the Forest bogs.

Right: Heath spotted orchids, a common sight on the heathlands during June.

Wild gladiolus growing deep in the bracken and now restricted to the New Forest.

Vixen and cubs, often well fed on a diet of grey squirrels.

Fallow bucks, with antlers in velvet, enjoying the easy life of summer.

The kingfisher, a colourful but elusive bird of the streams.

The rare Dartford warbler is an area specialty and the prize of many a visiting birdwatcher.

The silver-washed fritillary is a butterfly often seen on bramble flowers in woodlands during July.

Right: Common on the gorse in May, but often overlooked is the green hairstreak.

The silver-studded blue is the most familiar of the summer heathland butterflies.

forgotten, or perhaps not known, that an adder will only bite when catching prey or in self-defence and even if an accident does occur, and it gets a clean strike with a full venom sac, a serious reaction is very unusual. Indeed statistics indicate that there is more danger as a result of a bee sting or being struck by lightning than from an adder. A bit of common sense and not plunging a hand into the unseen depths of a heather clump is all that is required. In fact despite being so common, adders are rarely seen unless a special effort is made.

Fortunately, recognising the three snake species is quite easy. The adder, although quite variable in colour has the distinctive zig-zag pattern down its back and is only some twenty to twenty-four inches long. Occasionally an all black specimen will be seen where the black zig-zag pattern is all but invisible, but this is so unusual as to be unmistakable. Grass snake colouring is always a pale olive with a distinctive yellow or pale band across the back of the neck. At a length of up to three and a half feet they are imposing though completely harmless and are very much associated with damp places and will often be seen swimming. The last of the three, which is even less likely to be seen because of its rarity and shy, retiring habits is the smooth snake. They are slim, even graceful and, as a result, look longer than their usual two feet or so. There are some markings along the back but it is the all dark crown of the head which is quite unlike the adder. Because of their secretive habits the numbers of them are uncertain, but around 2,000 on all the southern heathlands seems to be fairly generally agreed.

Deer and other Mammals

Although containing a much wider range of species, the mammals, with some exceptions, are generally not very numerous in the Forest and in some instances are equally as elusive as the reptiles.

Small mammals such as mice and voles are not very common particularly on the open forest where adequate ground cover is often lacking. Similarly, stoats and weasels are few and scattered because of the unsuitability of much of the habitat. Evidence of mole activity can be found in some of the old woodlands and occasionally on some of the streamside lawns, but the general lack of earth worms in the often acid open forest soils results in most of the mole activity being associated with the cultivated land. And this is usually the case with the limited number of hedgehogs.

Rabbits are occurring in ever increasing numbers despite the evidence of myxomatosis still being about, that at one time resulted in a mortality rate of up to ninety-nine per cent. They can be found in a whole range of habitats and often in sufficient numbers for control to be necessary. The hare, which has never been particularly numerous has been in decline for a number of years for reasons which are not at all clear. In their wisdom the authorities are still allowing the hare to be hunted and it is to be hoped that this will not result in a repeat of the otter story. Rather more than a hundred years ago otter numbers were sufficient for a full time otter pack to operate in the Forest. But as numbers declined the pack was disbanded and for a few years this was replaced by a regular annual visit by an out of area pack until, as numbers declined still further, even this proved not worthwhile. Today otters are rarely seen in the Forest other than for odd individuals crossing the area and one or perhaps two which have survived for a few years on privately owned water. And with their liking for peace and quiet it seems unlikely that their numbers will ever increase as the modern Forest is just too busy throughout the year.

Unlike the great majority of other mammal species, little is known of the bat population in the Forest. Thirteen of the fifteen native species have been recorded and although practically nothing is known of their numbers, it is assumed that they are experiencing a serious decline as elsewhere in the country. Some small experimental bat box schemes have been tried in some of the conifer areas but with negligible success which is probably due to the wealth of natural sites available in the old woodland areas. But with a growing interest in bats generally, perhaps some studies of their status in the Forest will eventually be undertaken.

The grey squirrel is an introduced species that has found the area very much to its liking since first being recorded in the 1930's at a time when the red squirrel was still to be seen. Such was its success that within a dozen years, by 1947, the red squirrels had all gone, probably as a result of a periodic viral infection coinciding with the rapid rise in the grey population rather than actually being killed off by them. Today, although the red squirrel can be seen on the Isle of Wight and on Brownsea Island, the greys have the Forest to themselves and have become so numerous as to require control to limit the damage caused to trees. Apart from the control by the keepers, as a result of spending up to three-quarters of their time on the ground, a large number of grey squirrels are taken by the local foxes. Indeed it does seem likely that as the squirrel population fluctuates with the abundance or otherwise of the mast, this has an effect on the success of the fox breeding.

Compared to other areas, the fox population in the Forest is not very high and has been calculated at some 0.75 to the square kilometre or about three hundred individuals. Although they will occasionally be spotted, the most likely time to see them is in May and June when they range far and wide in their search for food for the cubs. In addition to taking birds, grey squirrels and other expected prey, in one or two instances, particularly in earths near Lyndhurst village, the remains of fish and chip packages are not uncommon. This either says much for their resourcefulness or, more likely, the pressures of feeding a large family.

The long evenings of May, June and July are also a good time to see the badgers which, like the foxes, tend to be more widespread than particularly abundant. With the February born cubs first emerging from late April and the whole family often out by 7.00 to 7.30 pm, badger watching is becoming increasingly popular. But with a good number of abandoned setts about often being used by rabbits or perhaps the odd fox, some checking for badger signs is advisable if a wasted evening is to be avoided. However many of the setts are traditional and have been continually in use for decades if not centuries. Gerald Lascelles, who was Deputy Surveyor in the Forest from 1880 to 1915, records having badgers turned out from the grounds of Queen's House in Lyndhurst at the turn of the century for reasons that were not mentioned. Almost a hundred years later, during the 1980's, the local keeper was again turning out the badgers from the self same area because

Field mice and other small mammals are not particularly numerous.

of the number being killed on the busy village roads. Whether with setts or tracks, tradition is important for badgers and this sometimes proves their downfall as the countryside changes with new roads being developed and railway lines electrified.

The deer are particularly associated with the Forest. There are five species to be found although one, the muntjac, can almost be discounted as it is so unusual – indeed some still doubt they occur in the Forest at all. With being so small and having a liking for thick cover, it is not surprising that they are overlooked.

Of the remaining four, roe deer are different in a number of ways. Being territorial rather than social they are usually only seen one or two at a time and even then, more often than not, as just a fleeting glimpse in the depths of the woodland. More reliable watching requires a little effort and being out and about at either dusk or dawn when they often venture out on the more open areas to feed. In addition, their rutting takes place in July or August rather than during the autumn and equally unusually, the bucks cast their antlers in November or December and regrow a new set of antlers during the winter months rather than casting in the spring and regrowing a new set in the summer when food is plentiful. No doubt roe are only able to regrow their antlers during the winter because they are so small and require little in the way of extra food resources especially when compared to the other deer species.

The remaining three species, fallow, red and sika, all share a number of habits in common. Being sociable they are usually seen in groups or herds and all the males cast their antlers in the spring and regrow a new and usually larger set in readiness for the rut in autumn which, for the deer watcher, is probably the most interesting and exciting time of all. From the second half of September to early November activity is at its peak when the groaning of the fallow bucks can be heard echoing through the woodlands and, to the south of the main railway line, the eerie whistling of the sika stags. Despite rutting on the open heathland, signs of red deer activity are not easy to find other than in a handful of traditional areas, reflecting the fact that there are only some eighty individuals to be found in the Forest.

Outside the breeding season red deer can also be quite elusive although small groups of hinds will often be encountered somewhere on the large heathland area running south-east between Longwater Bottom and Yew Tree Heath or on the scattered heathland areas running north from Aldridge-hill to the A35 road.

In contrast the sika deer, an introduced species originating as escapees from the Beaulieu estate at the turn of the century, are restricted to the south-east corner of the Forest and are reputed never to wander north of the main railway line. There are now some two hundred of them concentrated on the complex of inclosures at Frame Heath, Studley, Hawkhill and Lady-cross. Part of this area is closed to the public because of a deer research programme but even so, a visit at almost any time of the day or the year to the general area will invariably bring its rewards.

The last of these three species, and by far the most common with some twelve hundred individuals, is the fallow. The does are most likely to be seen due to their habit of spending much time grazing in the open areas where they will persist all day provided it remains reasonably undisturbed. In consequence, the quieter heathland valleys and some of the more remote

Sika hind, an introduced species now well established.

lawns are often good places to see them. Although easily spotted on the lawns, during the winter their rather dark and subdued coat colour does blend in particularly well with the heather. In summer their much paler and spotted coat can make them equally difficult to see in the dappled sunlight of the woodlands – and all too often the first indication is as they move briskly away in the opposite direction.

The other deer species also undergo a seasonal colour change, usually from dull and quite subdued in the winter to rather lighter and brighter in the summer, but the fallow can also be seen in other colours. White fallow are not uncommon and readily mix with, and are accepted by, the other members of the herd. For the deer watcher they are quite useful as, being easily seen, they are often the first indication that deer are about. Another variation is the menil where the coat is heavily spotted and much paler even

than the normal summer coat and where the normal black markings associated with the tail are missing. In retaining this very pale colouring
throughout the year, the menils are almost as noticeable as the whites. At
the other extreme is the melanistic fallow where the coat is so dark as to be
almost black but, compared to the others, these are few and far between.

The generally increasing awareness of the natural world has proved to
be a mixed blessing for the deer especially during the rutting season when
over-enthusiastic watchers often cause disturbance. During one October
morning recently, over forty people were counted coming to see one fallow
rutting area with a number of them causing the deer to move. Although
seemingly completely engrossed in their activities, the does remain as aware
as ever and a careless approach will invariably lead to disturbance. It is far
better to keep down-wind and at some distance using a pair of binoculars and
perhaps having an incomplete view, than to try and get too close and having
no view at all. Excessive disturbance has already resulted in one rutting area
being experimentally closed to the public and it would be a great shame if it
was thought necessary to continue or even extend the experiment.

Butterflies, Dragonflies and other Insects

With some thousands of different species insects are by far the largest
group although, because of identification difficulties, many remain more in
the realm of the specialist than the general naturalist. But there are exceptions. Among the fifteen hundred or so beetles found in the Forest the largest
of them, the stag beetle, is particularly common and noticeable on warm June
evenings. Indeed with its almost three inches long body hanging at an angle
of forty-five degrees its buzzing, laboured flight is as unmistakable as it is
apparently uncontrolled. The key to its local success is the amount of
decaying timber available as food for the larva. In consequence of this not
particularly nutritious diet, the larva can take anything up to five years before
reaching its full four to five inch length.

The old woodlands are also the home of the hornet, the largest and most
imposing of the wasp family. Whilst also recognisable from sheer size,
although usually more associated with the coniferous areas, are the wood
ants with their huge nests which are often four feet high and even more
across. They are welcomed by the foresters for their pest control activities
but their large size and ability to discharge formic acid makes too close an
examination of their nest inadvisable. One of the rarest insects associated
with the woodlands is the New Forest Cicada the only representative of the
cicada family in the country, and found in just one or two Forest woodland
edge locations. With its larva spending many years developing underground,
and the adult stage only lasting for some six to eight weeks in May and June,
it can hardly be described as common or, at about one inch long, noticeable
either.

In some years, during the autumn especially, the results of the activities
of the gall wasp family are particularly noticeable on the oak trees. These tiny
insects, more resembling ants with wings than wasps, lay eggs on the oak in
both spring and autumn causing galls to develop. In the spring the ping-pong

Spangle and silk cushion galls on oak in autumn.

ball sized oak apples containing some twenty-five to thirty eggs each can be abundant, whilst the red coloured currant galls on the oak flowers are the result of another gall wasp species laying eggs. In the autumn a careful search of the underside of the oak leaves will often reveal spangle and pin cushion galls in vast numbers and very often on the same trees the unusually shaped knopper gall will be seen on the acorns. When the knopper gall was first discovered in the west country during the 1960's apparently having been imported on timber from the continent, such were the numbers on the acorns in some years that fears were expressed for the future of the oak and somewhat hasty predictions were made that the oak would be wiped out. But these expressed fears tended to overlook the fact that although knopper galls occur on the common oak in autumn, the insect causing them also needs the turkey oak growing somewhere nearby to use for their spring generation of eggs and that turkey oaks are not that common and are only found in the southern half of the country. With over forty gall wasp species causing galls in both spring and autumn on the common oak alone, there are a great range of gall sizes, shapes and colours to be seen.

Spiders, although not strictly insects, must be among the most common of all the invertebrates on the heathland where there are reputed to be more to the square yard than on any other type of habitat. In the summer the silk cocoons enclosing the white mass of eggs are commonly seen on the heather tops and gorse bushes, whilst a visit to any heathland on a misty late summer morning will reveal webs of all types in their tens of thousands. But if size is the criteria, then a visit to some of the bogs or flushes will be required to see the biggest of them, the raft spider. Dark coloured with two pale stripes, it can sometimes be seen patiently waiting on floating vegetation for some slight water disturbance to indicate that prey might be available. It is also alongside some of these bogs and flushes that the great marsh grasshopper, the largest of the native grasshoppers, might be seen.

But perhaps these and the other wet areas are most renowned for the dragonflies and damselflies. With twenty-seven of the thirty-eight native species, including some national rarities, the New Forest is one of the best areas in the country for this particular group. They can be seen on the wing from April to October, but the hot summer months of July and August are invariably the best. And although the watery areas are preferred – indeed they are essential for egg laying – both dragonflies and damselflies can be encountered well away from water out on the open heath and sometimes even in the middle of woodlands.

Along many of the streams the butterfly-like flight of groups of the metallic blue beautiful demoiselle are a common sight and often along the same streams the longest bodied of all the native dragonflies, the golden ringed can be seen purposefully patrolling up and down and periodically making use of favourite perches. The strong flying hawkers including the emperor and southern hawker are found around a number of the ponds, whilst nationally uncommon species such as the small red, southern damsel-fly and scarce blue-tail are still widespread and readily encountered. Indeed on a hot, sunny July afternoon a dozen or more different species can often be seen in many of the favoured areas.

Unlike the dragonflies that appear to be holding their own, butterflies have declined in the Forest over the decades in much the same way as they have elsewhere in the country. But from reading some of the old literature, this is nothing new. Even in 1914, Frohawk, a well known expert on the subject, mentioned the decline of the silver-washed fritillary in the Forest which, some thirty years previously 'used to abound in such numbers that it was a usual occurrence to see as many as forty or fifty on a large bramble bush'. Today, although the Forest is considered to be one of the main strongholds for the species, seeing four or five on a single bramble is much nearer the mark. He also mentioned the decline of the wood white and large tortoiseshell in the Forest at that time, both of which have now completely disappeared, as indeed have one or two other species.

Traditionally it has been the inclosures rather than the open forest where the butterfly enthusiast has found greatest delight. Being fenced and with the stock excluded these areas have the best of the ground vegetation – including butterfly food plants. Whether or not the practice of throwing open many of the inclosures in recent years together with the more relaxed

Broad-bodied chasers like other dragonflies are vulnerable when first hatched.

attitude to turning out the stock which has managed to gain entry to some of the fenced inclosures has contributed to the butterfly decline is a matter of speculation. But it does seem a coincidence. For all the comparisons made with the past and complaints of decline, there are still some broadleaf dominated and fenced inclosures where butterflies can be found in good numbers – at least in modern terms. Pearl-bordered fritillaries can still be seen on the wing in May, but it is in July when the bramble is in flower that is best. Typical woodland species such as the white admiral and the silver-washed fritillary, including the variation valesina, are found in good numbers on a warm afternoon together with many of the more common species such as gatekeeper, meadow brown, ringlet and the fast flying skippers. With odd comma, brimstone, peacock and the like and perhaps the odd purple hair-streak dropping down from the oaks, ten or more species in the same area is still common.

The heathland similarly has interest with the attractive silver-studded blue being by far the most common species with numbers being most impressive in some areas in a good year. Small heath and small copper are both common as is the green hairstreak earlier in the season and the grayling rather later.

In recognition of the butterfly problem, the Forestry Commission have already taken action to widen a number of rides in the inclosures to allow in more light for the ground vegetation to develop and perhaps with a few more of the inclosures being fully fenced the butterfly populations might well start to regain some of their former glory.

The goldcrest and other unexpected birds regularly breed in the gorse.

Birds of Heath, Wood and Bog

The best known of all the birds associated with the Forest is the Dartford warbler. This small, often elusive species inhabits the gorsy areas of the heath where, more often than not, the only sign of its presence is the low pitched churr of its alarm call. Living mainly on a diet of spiders and in such a potentially inhospitable environment, bad winters can have a severe effect on their numbers. Following the harsh winter of 1962-63, barely two dozen individuals survived, but since that time the population has gradually increased and despite a few setbacks numbers are now estimated at between 450 and 500 pairs making it surprisingly common for a listed rare bird.

Both linnet and stonechat breed in these gorse areas together with a number of more common though unexpected species such as blackbird, chaffinch, goldcrest, long-tailed tit, song thrush, redpoll and even pied wagtail all of which find the prickly and seemingly uninviting gorse quite acceptable as nest sites. Where the ground cover is shorter and more open, skylark enliven the scene, but it is the meadow pipit which is by far the most common during both winter and summer.

On other parts of the heathland whinchat are found on some of the bracken slopes and an increasing number of wheatear on the old airfield areas such as Beaulieu Heath and Stoney Cross and quite often on the recently burnt areas where the charred gorse skeletons provide perches and the rabbit holes nest sites. The call of the cuckoo can be heard from the isolated scots pine where they perch patiently searching the surrounding heath for suitable meadow pipit nests to act as hosts for their eggs. Carrion crows can similarly often be seen in the isolated pines searching for nests only in their case it is to take the contents rather than add to them. Overhead in summer hawking hobby are a familiar sight and distinguished from the similarly sized but more common kestrel by the all dark upper surface rather than just dark coloured wing tips. But perhaps most evocative of all, just as dusk is falling, is the churring and wing clapping of the nightjar which can still be found in reasonable numbers.

On the wetter parts of the heath and the bogs breeding waders are noisily noticeable from early spring. Lapwing, redshank and snipe are all widespread as are the curlew whose numbers have increased considerably during this century. On some of the old runways at Beaulieu Heath, ringed plover still find the habitat suitable for nesting and make strange bedfellows

when seen near the breeding Dartford warbler at the runway edge. A few pairs of shelduck and teal fly in to breed each season and on some of the ponds such as Eyeworth and Cadman's Pool Canada geese breed. Otherwise the ponds are the haunt of the more common coot, moorhen and mallard except at Sowley where the great crested grebe find sufficient peace and quiet to raise their young as do the herons in the trees at the edge of the pond – nowadays the only heronry left in the forest.

Swallows. The privately owned land gives an added dimension to the wildlife.

The streams are the home of the kingfisher although their numbers are not quite so high as the amount of apparently suitable water would indicate. From the length of stream many of them seem to require as breeding territories, adequate supplies of food is, in every likelihood, the main constraint. In contrast there are usually over eighty pairs of grey wagtail breeding on the Forest streams in a normal year despite their breeding activities being mainly restricted to the streams running through broadleaf woodland. The good number of small bridges with suitable ledges beneath and wealth of well covered stream banks provide ample choice of nest site. Whilst the number of exposed gravel banks in the streams and nearby off-stream muddy areas provide sufficient food for breeding territories often to be quite small and for two and very often three broods to be successfully raised each year.

There is also interest outside the breeding season. During the winter the buoyant, almost hovering flight of the hunting hen harrier over the heaths is familiar and in a few areas – traditionally including Leaden Hall and Shatterford – the great grey shrike is sometimes to be found, and the lucky few might even catch a glimpse of a passing merlin. In exceptionally bad weather Sowley Pond often supports a great number of waterfowl and even the more mundane flight of the large winter roost of jackdaws near Beaulieu Road Station can make an impressive sight – and sound – just as dusk is falling.

Passage birds are generally few but yellow wagtails can be seen most years in April and again in August on a number of streamside lawns such as Longwater. Spring also often brings a few pied flycatchers but reliable reports of any staying to breed are rare. As elsewhere in the country oddments do turn up from time to time and no doubt in such a large area as the Forest many go unnoticed. During the 1980s there were reports of hoopoe, golden oriole and breeding two-barred crossbill, whilst towards the coast, although of uncertain origin, both cattle egret and spoonbill were noted.

The birds of the old woodlands are dominated by hole and crevice nesting species. All three woodpeckers are to be found including the elusive lesser-spotted which, with its habit of spending so much time high in the canopy, is perhaps best seen during the breeding season. Many of the nest holes made by these three very different sized woodpeckers provide suitable nest sites for a whole range of other species in subsequent years. The various members of the tit family, nuthatch, redstart and starling commonly take advantage and even the grey squirrel often finds old green woodpecker holes large enough to raise a family. With tawny owls in natural holes, treecreeper taking advantage of the splits and cracks caused by winter storms, jackdaw and all the rest, it is small wonder that these old woodland areas are so greatly valued.

The cooing of the stockdove and attractive two part song of the wood warbler all mixed in with the amazingly diverse background chorus which is

so typical of these areas makes a dawn walk though any of the old woodlands in May an uncomfortably early but unforgettable experience. But for many the main attraction is the more unusual species. The top of Acres Down with its panoramic views of the extensive woodlands below is a favourite spot for the watcher armed with binoculars and telescope searching for signs of birds of prey as they display in the spring. Honey buzzard are still to be found together with perhaps the odd goshawk in addition to the two dozen or so common buzzard. The kestrel and especially the sparrowhawk are common and with the heathland species such as hobby, hen harrier and merlin, the birds of prey are quite well represented throughout the year.

The hawfinch, although seemingly quite widespread, can prove elusive and is perhaps most easily seen feeding on the hornbeam seed in autumn. At the woodland edges where the trees are more open and shading into heath, the tree pipit's parachuting display is a familiar spring sight and the woodlark still retains its stronghold with its distinctive song heard surprisingly early in the season.

Although overlooked by many, the coniferous areas have their own particular interest with both breeding siskin and crossbill and, in one or two areas where mature conifers and broadleaf are mixed, breeding firecrest. This diminutive bird was first discovered breeding in the Forest in the 1960s, near the Deer Sanctuary, and now appears to be well established.

Plant Life both Common and Rare

Among the more specialist groups, lichen, especially those associated with trees, are particularly abundant with over three hundred species recorded, including a number confined to the area, making the Forest one of the most important areas in the country for this little known group. Ferns are similarly widespread with common species such as the hard fern being regularly seen and, in some areas, the impressively large royal fern. Of the more readily recognisable, moonwort occurs in a number of grassy areas with a large colony next to one of the old runways on Beaulieu Heath, whilst adder's tongue occurs in similar areas but never seemingly with the same vigorous growth.

With over a thousand species recorded, fungi are a large and noticeable group mainly – although not entirely – associated with the autumn woodlands. Unfortunately in recent years the growing popularity of collecting for the table, sometimes on a commercial basis, gives the erroneous impression in some areas that only unpalatable or poisonous species are to be found growing. Excessive collecting in some continental countries over the years has already led to a serious decline and it is to be hoped that the authorities will find some method of stopping the same story being repeated in the Forest. But there is still much to be seen and locally organised 'fungus forays' will regularly find over a hundred different species on a half day outing.

The familiar red fly agaric usually found growing near birch and the shiny white caps of the porcelain fungi on the dead beech are both particularly noticeable in the woodlands. On the heath, often after a burn, the yellow

Heath violets are not quite so common as expected.

brain fungi is found on many of the gorse skeletons, whilst towards the edge of the heath parasol fungi sometimes attain a cap size of eight to ten inches across. This great range of fungi set against a background of turning leaf colour, foraging pigs and rutting deer makes autumn one of the most attractive of all the seasons in the Forest.

Although not an area generally thought of for orchids, a number do occur, some quite unexpectedly, and including one nationally rare species. Alongside some of the minor roads passing beneath broadleaf woodland, broad-leaved helleborine is to be found and in some woodlands, the bird's-

Fly agaric, one of over a thousand different fungus species found in the Forest.

nest orchid. Completely lacking in chlorophyll, this rather dull yellow flower can be difficult to spot growing in the dappled shade of newly opened leaves in May. But the quite firm structure of the dead flower spike does persist well into the following winter when, with the leaves gone from the trees and the woodland floor more exposed, it is easier to pin-point.

Of the spotted orchids, the heath spotted is very common and widespread but the common spotted far less so. In the short grassy areas, autumn lady's tresses are common and the lesser butterfly-orchid is often found growing under a sparse cover of bracken. A few twayblade are also to be seen and, in at least one area next to a main road, a few spikes of the singularly attractive bee orchid. The heathland expanse of Beaulieu Heath is the unexpected home for a good number of green-winged orchid, a few early purple and, later in the year, fragrant orchid. The colour of this latter species being so similar to the flowering heather that it is often overlooked, and, growing in such an unusual situation, this is not surprising.

The deep red flowers of the early marsh orchid are common in many of the bogs and in some areas the white form is almost as numerous. In the extreme south of the Forest small colonies of the beautiful marsh helleborine can be found in one or two of the hillside flushes, but the great rarity is the bog orchid. This tiny, pale green, insignificant little orchid has its main stronghold in the Forest but requires a keen and practised eye to see it. Indeed being so inconspicuous and growing in such difficult boggy situations, a good number appear to get trampled by otherwise well-meaning people in their search for it.

The wet areas generally provide a wealth of fascination. Bog asphodel are found on many bogs and in some, such as the bog in the middle of Fawley Inclosure, the blaze of yellow flowers completely carpets the bog and appears even more vivid against the dark green of the surrounding conifers.

Insectivorous sundews are also widespread with the round-leaved being found in the damp areas, the long-leaved where it is rather wetter and the unusual greater sundew generally being restricted to the wettest – and most inaccessible – areas of all. The tiny pale butterwort and lesser bladderwort occur, whilst other plants that are becoming unusual elsewhere such as the bog pimpernel and marsh gentian still thrive in good numbers as does the delicate ivy-leaved bellflower.

In the old woodlands, despite all the interest afforded by the lower plant groups, the wild flowers are limited. Old woodland indicators such as wood spurge and butcher's broom are quite widespread but other species vary a lot from one area to another. Foxgloves provide the best display as, being poisonous, they are avoided by the stock and deer. Rather weak looking bluebells are to be found with the best of them generally in the inclosures which applies to a number of species. One in particular, the rare narrow-leaved lungwort is associated with some inclosures in the south of the Forest. Only to be found in the north of the Isle of Wight and one or two areas in Dorset, they can be found growing on the sides of the ditches alongside the inclosures. But flowering in April the blue colour does tend to blend in with the violets and with sometimes being under a light scrubby cover, they are easy to miss. Apart from these, it is usually the spring flowers such as the wood anenome, wood sorrel, and cellandine that provides most of the limited amount of colour.

On the heathland the common heather or ling is the dominant plant with both bell heather and, in the damper areas, cross-leaved heather also commonly found. Similarly, the large and aptly named common gorse is dominant but with both the dwarf and western gorse also occurring. The gorse-like member of the broom family, the petty whin is common in the damper areas as is the lousewort, whilst throughout the heathland tormentil, milkwort and, to a lesser extent, heath violet are all to be found mixed in with the heathers. But the plant of the open areas is the wild gladiolus which is restricted to the Forest and usually associated with the areas of bracken. Despite growing to a height of twelve inches or more and being bright crimson-purple, its preferred habitat makes it yet another species difficult to spot – by people as well as stock – which is perhaps just as well for its continued survival.

Finally, no mention of the Forest would be complete without the trees. A group which is again so diverse, thanks partly to introductions, that only a hint of the range of interest can be given. In the old woods, oak, both common and sessile, together with the beech are the main species and these are often accompanied, depending on area, by holly, blackthorn and sometimes field maple. Crab apple and cherry are widespread as indeed is hawthorn and silver birch. Other oak species such as turkey and red oak are to be found as are ash, hornbeam, whitebeam, wild service and yew. Indeed there is a very wide range of species many of which are represented by only a limited number of individual trees or which occur only in certain areas.

There are still a good number of fine trees to be found in the Bolderwood Arboretum despite the havoc wrought by the storms of 1987 and 1990, and included among both the conifers and broadleaves are some of the best specimens found anywhere in the country. Nearby, and just to the south of Bolderwood Cottage, there are some magnificent deodar cedar the remains of an experimental planting dating from 1861.

Over the years it has been the practice to plant uncommon trees in a number of inclosures either as individual trees or as small experimental groups. As a result, species ranging from Japanese red cedar to roble beech can be found with careful searching.

In many ways this great variety of trees is representative of the Forest wildlife as a whole in containing both common and rare species and requiring visits to all parts of the Forest to fully appreciate the range available.

Fallow are the most common of the Forest deer.

APPENDIX I

ACCIDENTS INVOLVING COMMONERS' STOCK 1992

Fatalities		**Injuries**	
Ponies	96	Ponies	31
Cattle	8	Cattle	13
Donkeys	4	Donkeys	4
Pigs	1	Pigs	1
Sheep	6	Sheep	-
	115		49

Total killed and injured	164
Accidents at night	118
Local motorists involved	80
Accidents not reported	53

The sad toll for 1992, the year in which the 40 mph speed limit was introduced throughout the New Forest.

APPENDIX II

STOCK DEPASTURED — FIVE YEARLY AVERAGES 1960-89 AND THREE YEAR AVERAGE 1990-92

	1960-64	1965-69	1970-74	1975-79	1980-84	1985-89	1990-92
Ponies	1974	2591	2976	3579	3083	3049	3524
Cattle	2651	1986	2083	2197	1800	1676	2014
Donkeys	10	6	29	98	98	80	80
Pigs	759	398	385	320	155	207	114
Sheep	-	-	29	28	5	-	208
	5394	4981	5502	6222	5141	5012	5940

APPENDIX III

SCHEDULE OF OPEN AND ACCUSTOMED MARL PITS
AND PLACES WITHIN THE NEW FOREST

Description	Name of Walk
The open and accustomed marl pits and places at Lyndhurst Hill	Iron's Hill
The like at Bank	Iron's Hill
The like called Oslemsley Ford, near the Christchurch Road Railway Station	Holmsley
The like called Old Hole near Levitt's Gate	Holmsley & Wilverley
The like at Hincheslea	Rhinefield
The like at or near Marl Pit Oak	Rhinefield
The like near the New Inn, Battramsley	Rhinefield
The like near Blackhamsley Hill	Rhinefield
The like near Sway	Wilverley
The like near Broadley	Wilverley
The like at Crockfield	Lady Cross
The like at Two Bridges	Lady Cross
The like at Monkey Horn & Sheepwash	Lady Cross
The like near Dilton	Lady Cross
The like at Frogmoor	Lady Cross
The like at Greenmoor	Lady Cross
The like at Hatchett Pond	Lady Cross
The like at Hollands Wood	Whitley Ridge
The like at Sandydown, opposite Hayward Mill	Whitley Ridge
The like near Brockenhurst Mill	Whitley Ridge
The like near Windy Shoot	Boldrewood
The like at Acre's Down	Boldrewood
The like at Ferney Crofts	Denny

PHOTOGRAPHIC NOTE

The great majority of the photographs have been taken using Kodachrome 64 film with a limited number using Kodachrome 200. All have been taken with Nikon equipment, many using either a Zoom-Nikkor 28-50mm f3.5 or Micro-Nikkor 105mm f4 lens. In addition, and mainly for wildlife, a Nikkor ED 300mm f4.5 and Nikkor ED 600mm f5.6 lens is also used.

Cover photographs: Sika stag at Frame Heath Inclosure in November using 600mm.

SELECTED BIBLIOGRAPHY

Brough, P., Gibbon, B. and Pope, C. *The Nature of Hampshire and the Isle of Wight.* Barracuda. Buckingham. 1986.

Countryside Commission Report. *The New Forest Commoners.* 1984.

Edlin, H.L. (Ed). *New Forest, Forestry Commission Guide.* H.M.S.O. 1961.

Forestry Commission and Hampshire County Council. *Learning in the New Forest.* 1987.

Frohawk, F.W. *Natural History of British Butterflies.* Hutchinson. London. 1914.

Kenchington, F.E. *The Commoners' New Forest.* Hutchinson. London. 1944.

Lascelles, G. *Thirty-five Years in the New Forest.* Arnold. London. 1915.

Lewis, P. *The New Forest.* Payne. London. 1811.

Pasmore, A. *Verderers of the New Forest.* Pioneer. Beaulieu. 1976.

Stagg, D.J. *New Forest Documents 1244-1334.* Hampshire County Council. 1979.

Tubbs, C.R. *The New Forest.* Collins. London. 1986.

Webb, N. *Heathlands.* Collins. London. 1986.

Wise, J.R. *The New Forest.* Smith Elder. London. 1963.

ACKNOWLEDGEMENTS

I am grateful to the many people including commoners and keepers and other members of the Forestry Commission who have so patiently and freely given their time and knowledge over the years to help my understanding of the Forest.

My thanks also to Berry Stone for the line drawings and especially to Roger Newland, Forest Operations Manager for reading the text and for his helpful advice and comment.

The assistance of Gordon Young who first suggested the idea and David Graves who guided me through the mysteries of book production is greatly appreciated.

Finally, thanks must go to my wife Vivienne for encouragement and patient understanding of long hours spent with the camera and at the typewriter.

Terry Heathcote
Lyndhurst, Hampshire
August 1990